See you at Tom and Gerrie's Bed and Bagel in Vancouver, WA.

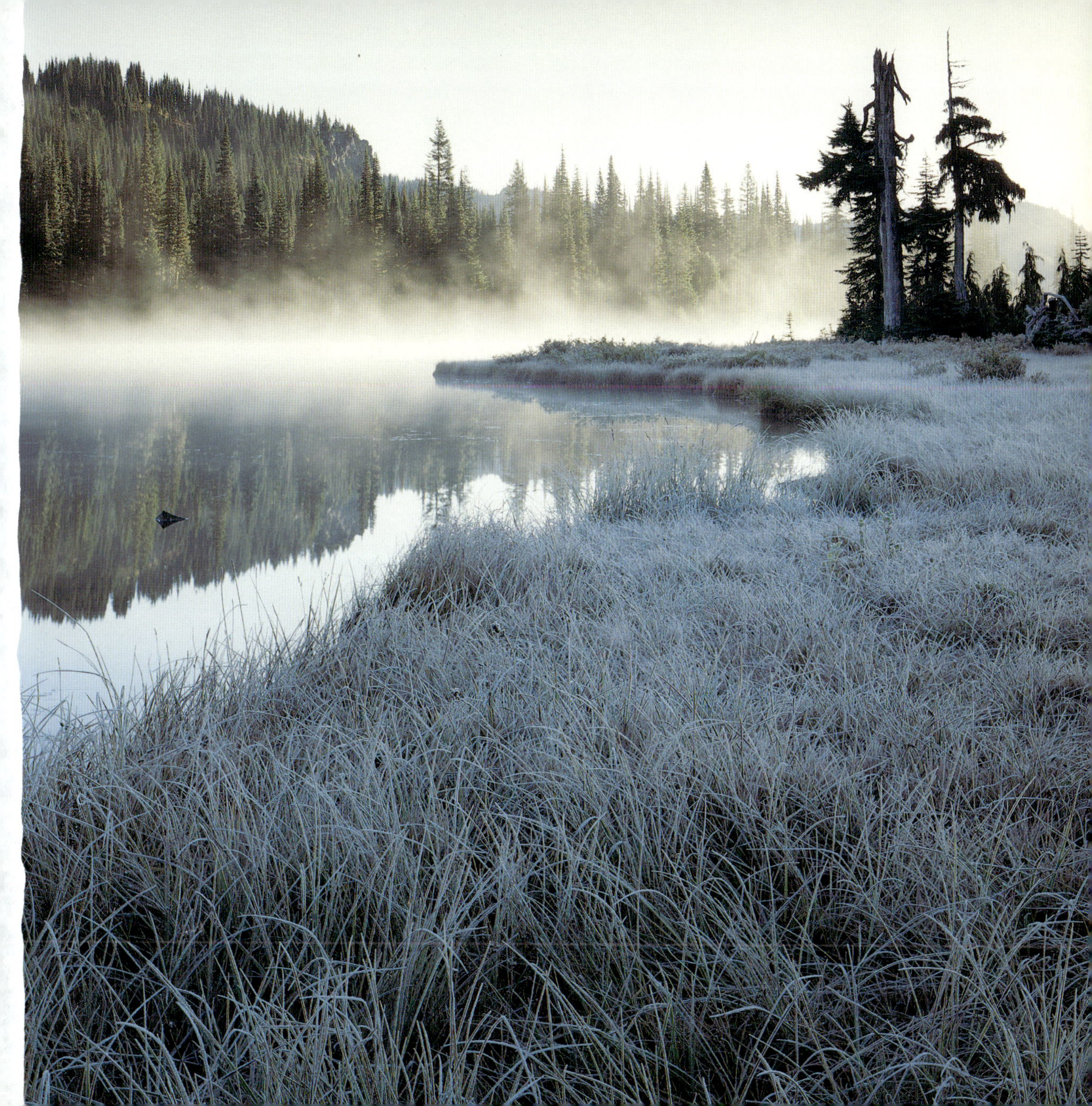

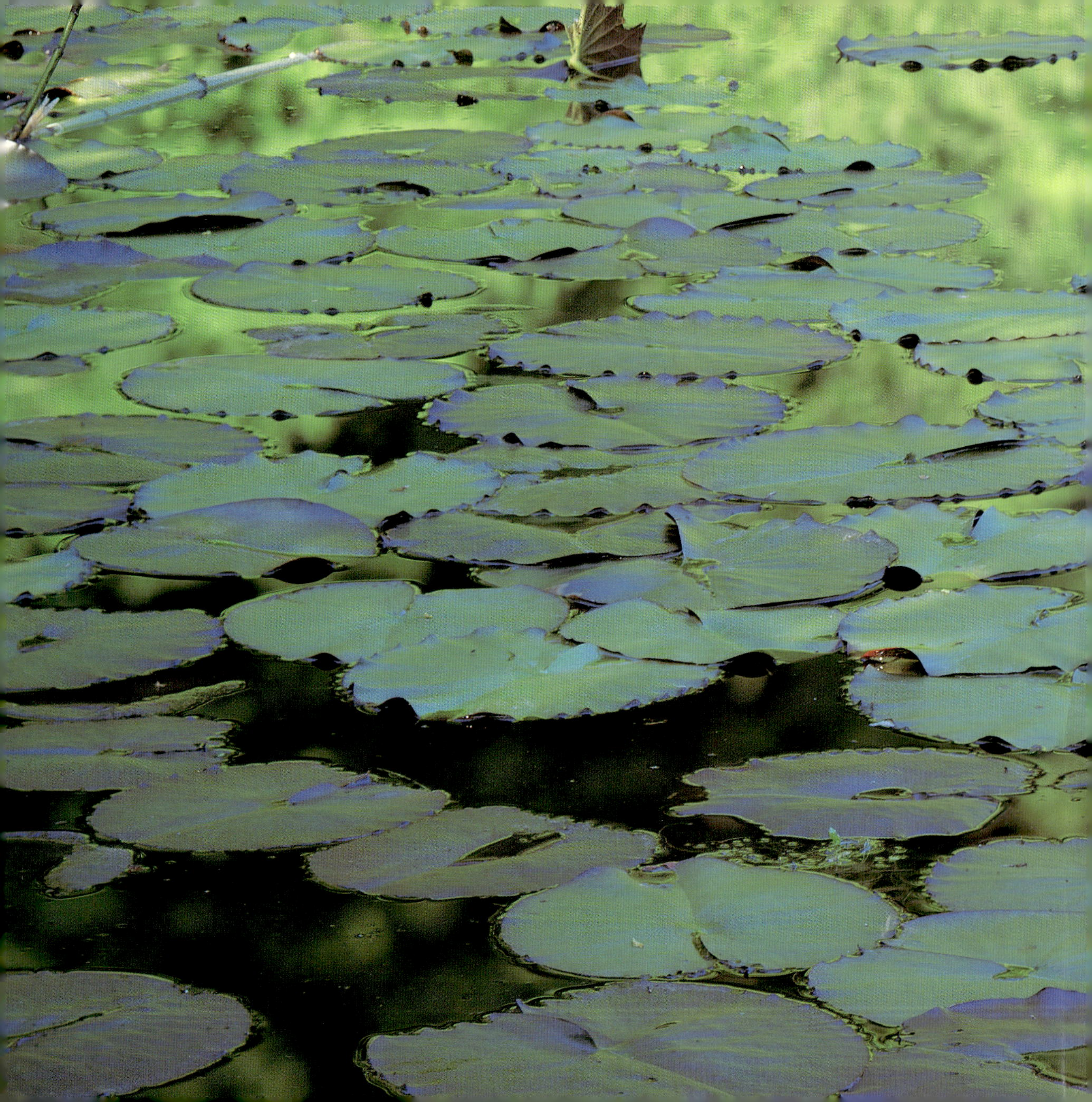

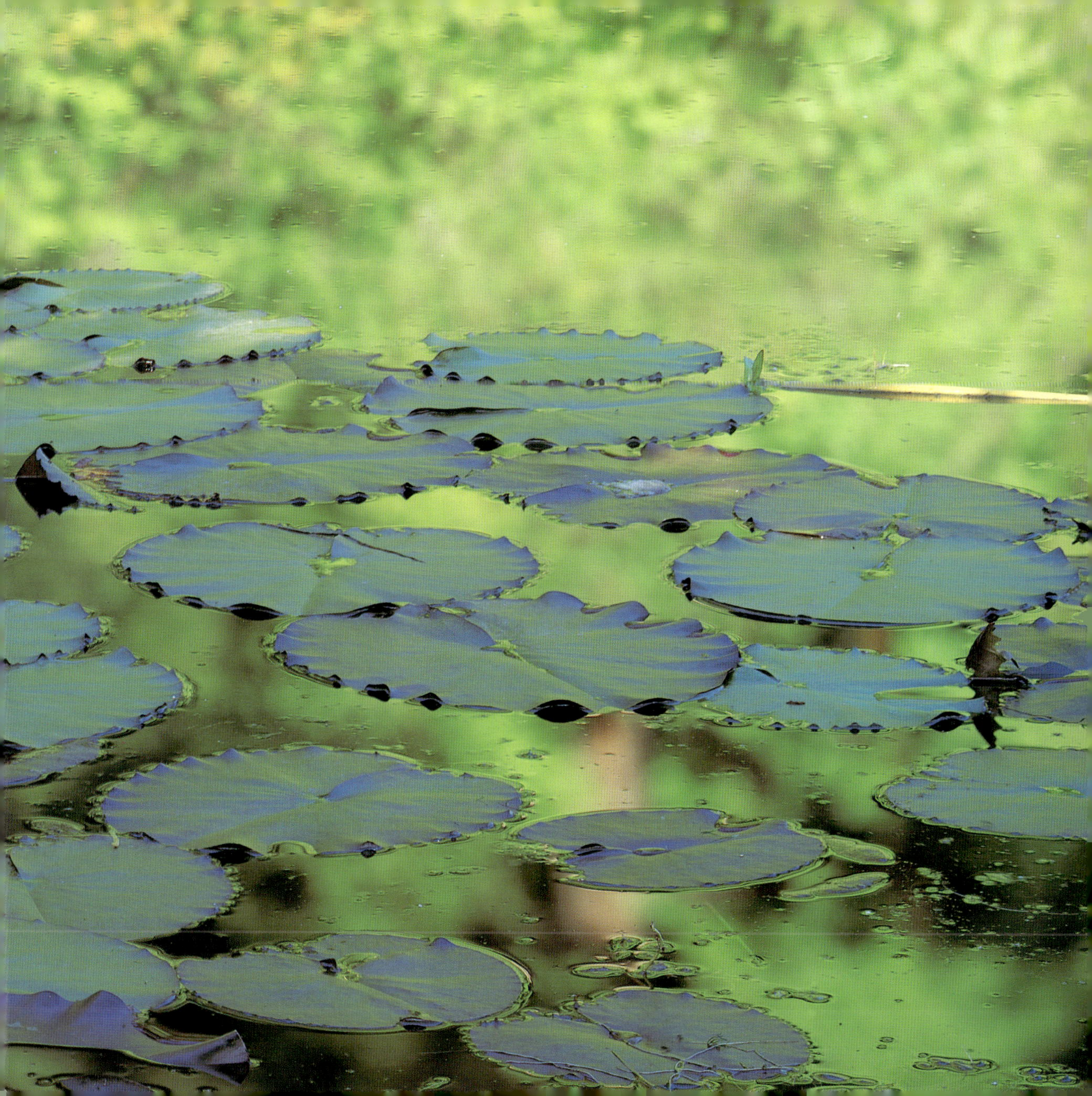

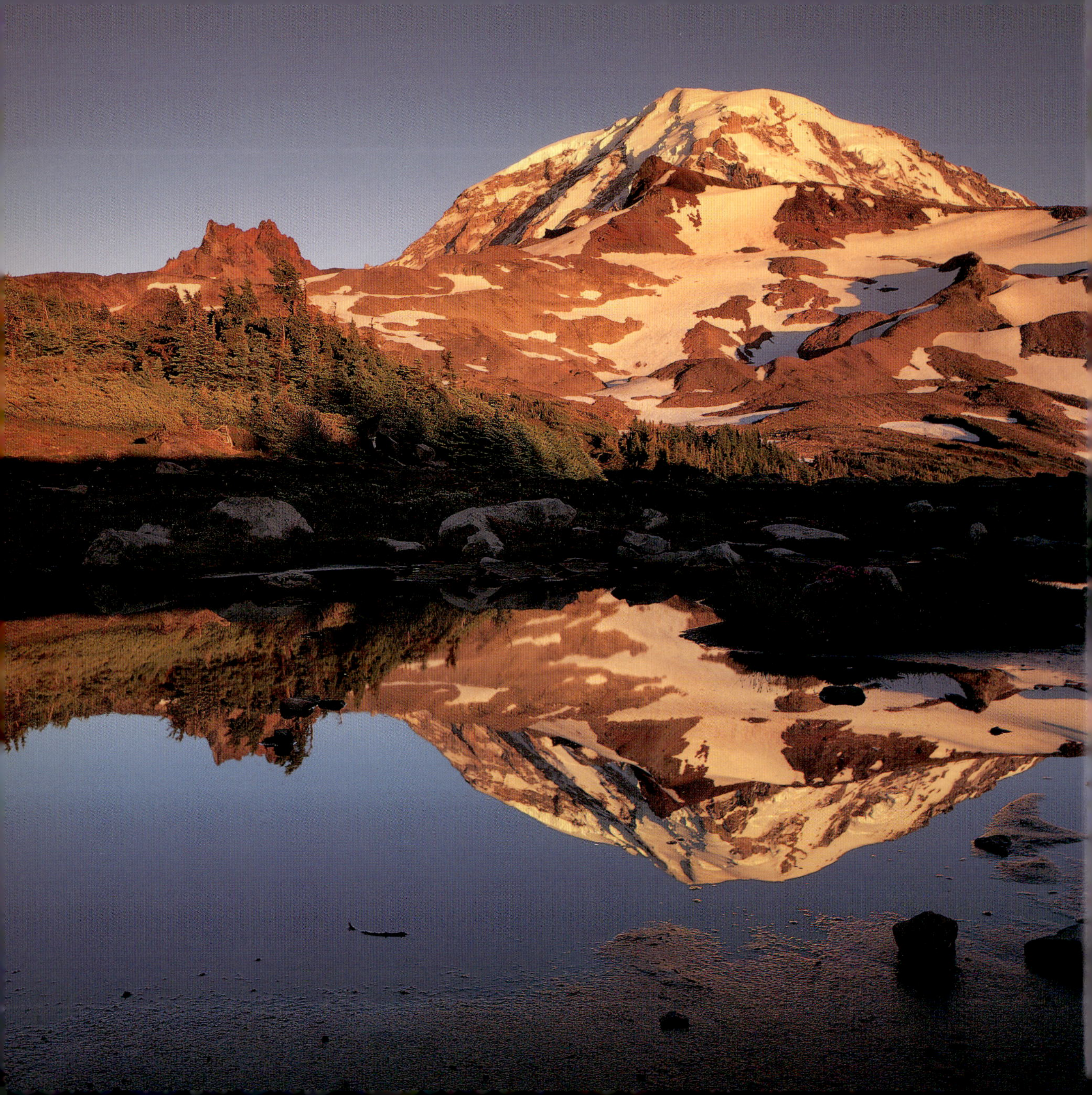

WASHINGTON REFLECTIONS

Photography by Charles Gurche
With Selected Prose & Poetry

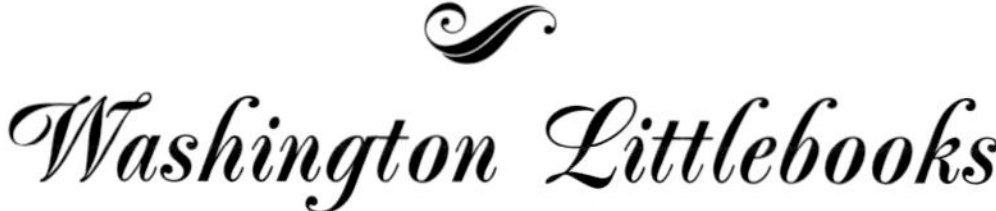

Westcliffe Publishers, Inc., Englewood, Colorado

To my brother John, for his inspiration in my work and in my life.

First frontispiece: Reflection Lake, Mount Rainier National Park
Second frontispiece: Water lily pond, Columbia River Gorge National Scenic Area
Third frontispiece: Mount Rainier, Mount Rainier National Park
Opposite: Low tide at dusk, Olympic National Park

International Standard Book Number: 1-56579-138-X
Library of Congress Catalog Number: 95-62430

Published by Westcliffe Publishers, Inc.
2650 South Zuni Street, Englewood, Colorado 80110
Publisher, John Fielder; Editor, Suzanne Venino; Designer, Amy Duenkel
Printed in Hong Kong by Palace Press

Original prints available, contact Charles Gurche
at 509-534-2783

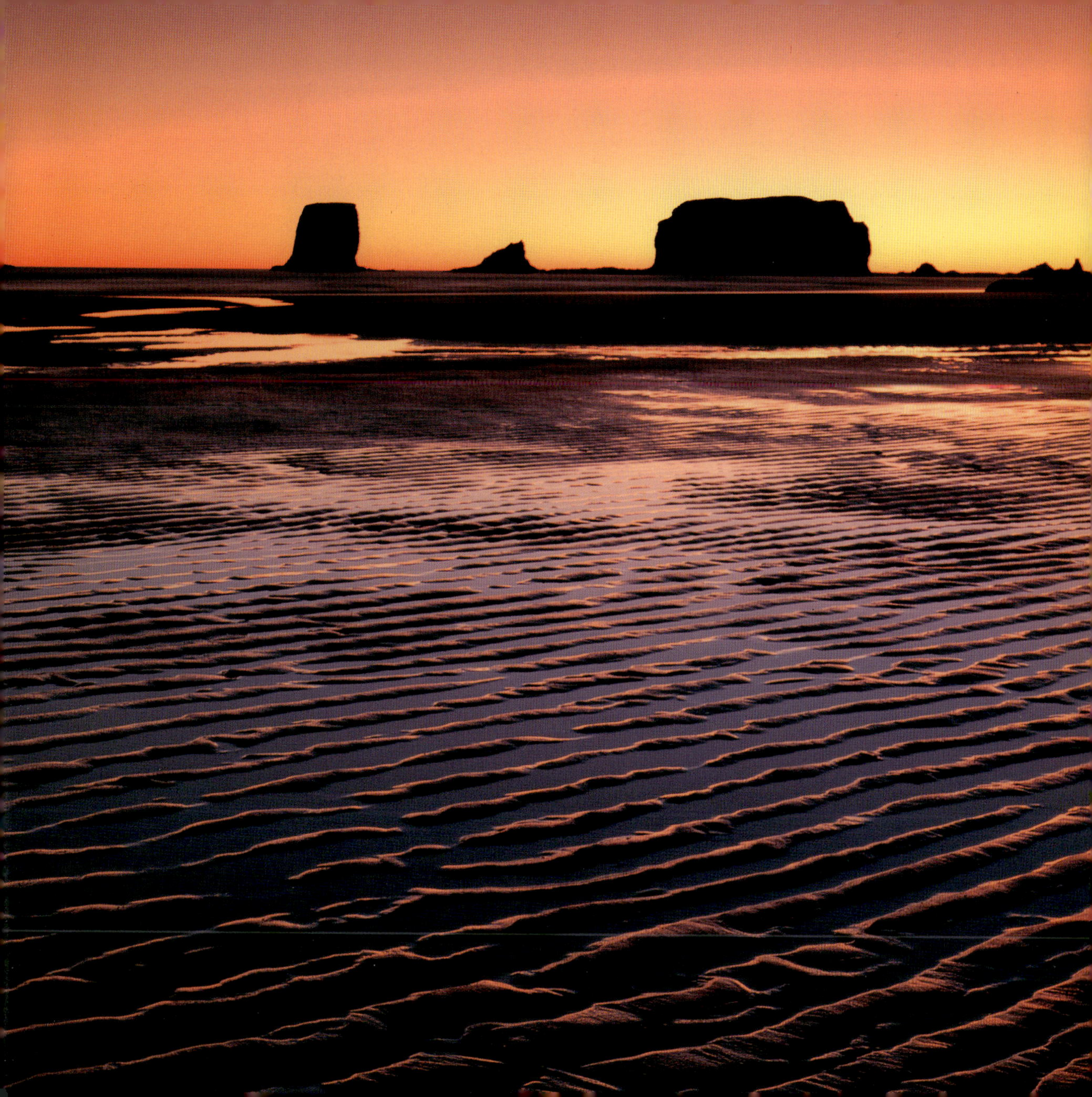

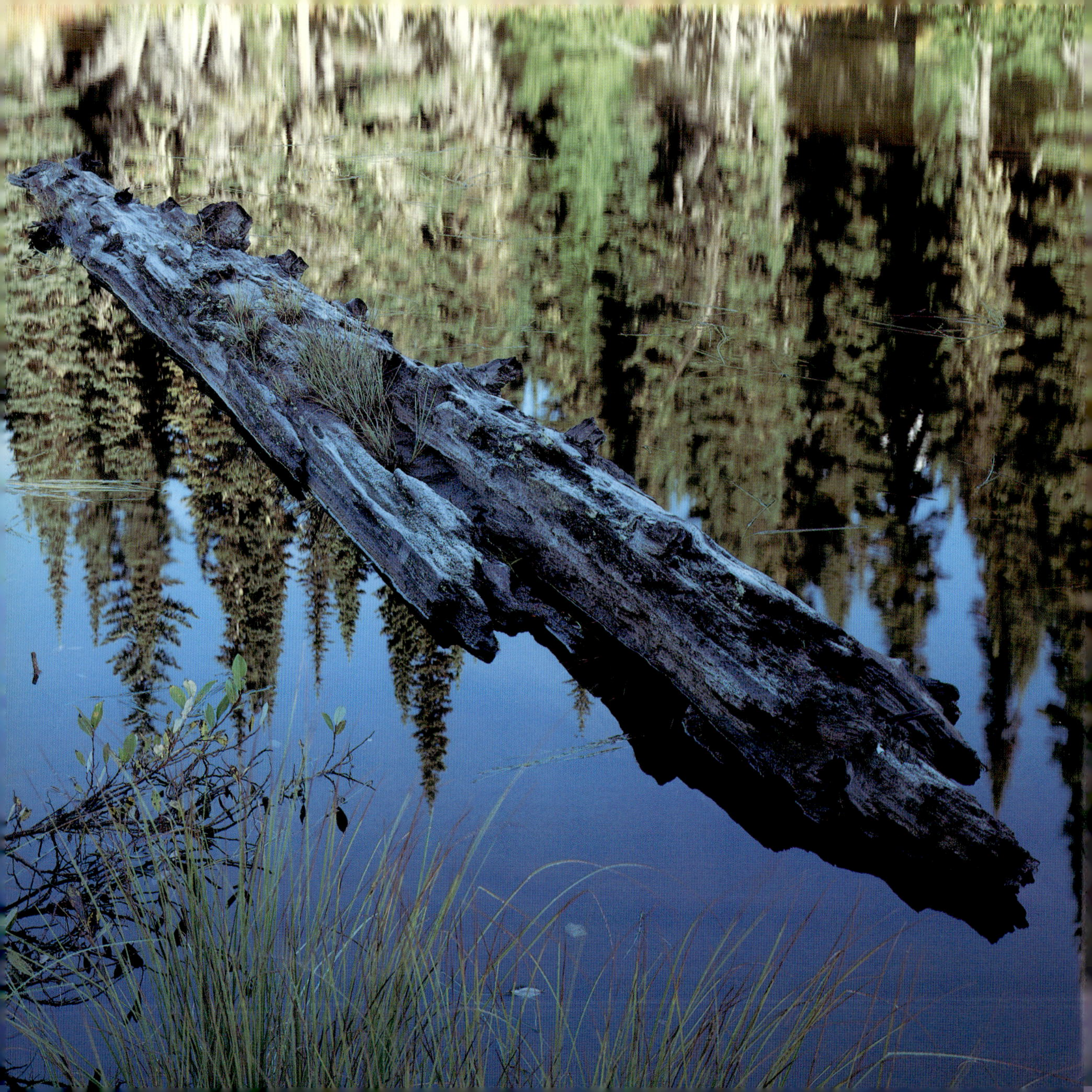

PREFACE

More than anything, water defines the character of the Northwest. In Washington, frequent rains drench the coastal and inland mountain forests much of the year, supporting massive trees, lush undergrowth, and abundant streams, lakes, and rivers. Along the coastline, water is in continuous motion. Whether peaceful or tumultuous, it sets the mood of the moment and creates the essence of the landscape.

Throughout Washington's history, waterways have played a significant role as major transportation routes. Populations of Native Americans followed and settled along rivers and shorelines, sustained by salmon, clams, the rich riparian vegetation and the wildlife it supported. Sir Francis Drake and other explorers sailed into straits and channels as they searched for the elusive Northwest Passage. Whalers passed the rugged capes and points of the Olympic Peninsula. Meriwether Lewis, William Clark, and later pioneers followed the free-flowing Snake and Columbia Rivers, with their steady currents, shifting sandbars, and ancient cottonwoods groves. Trappers and miners explored hundreds of tributaries in the high mountains. All of these frontiersmen likely shared a common reverence and appreciation for the pure and dynamic waters of Washington.

The appeal of water continues, drawing us to its shore. Today we hike along it, float it, paddle it, dive into it, and contemplate it. A path on the Olympic Peninsula meanders beneath towering spruce, cedar and fir trees, ending at a secluded coastline beach. At high tide, the force of the waves bobble ten-ton driftwood logs like bathtub toys. Water sculpts the cliffs, and continually replenishes thousands of tide pools. Stone beaches rattle like applauding crowds with the back-and-forth rhythm of the surf, each wave smoothing and rounding and polishing the stones.

Low tide reveals shallow pools that harbor wonderful lifeforms — starfish, anemones and myriad other shapes, sizes, and colors of sea life. Wide beaches emerge, the wet sand mirroring the sky and reflecting the sea stacks

Weathered log, Reflection Lake, Mount Rainier National Park

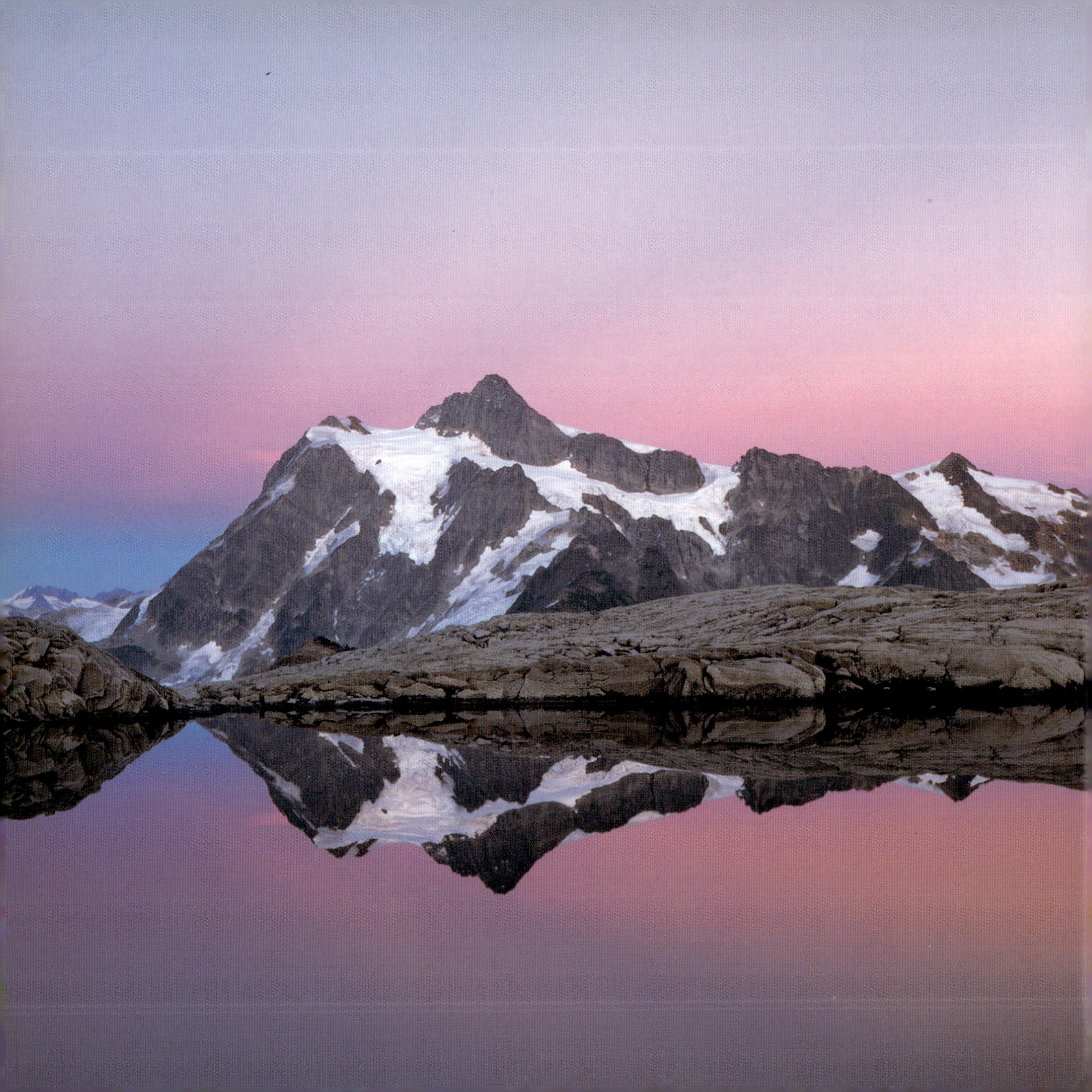

beyond. We are drawn to the movement of water, the forces at work, the changing sights, the rhythmic sounds. And when we can, we return again.

Three hundred miles away from the ocean, the waters of the Little Spokane River meander quietly through a small valley. Trout and whitefish swim in clear water above the sandy bottom. Great blue heron chicks peek from nests high in old cottonwoods, as their parents sound their prehistoric call. Ducks and turtles paddle among cattails and rushes. The shifting currents reflect a dance of color — of ponderosa pine, river birch, and iris blossoms, their reflections shimmering on the water.

On the flanks of Mount Rainier, small, blue lakes dot the forested slopes. Eunice Lake lies tucked away in a hanging valley in the northwest corner of the park. Although frozen much of the year, its waters reflect the sun's last rays that fall on Mount Rainier's 14,410-foot summit on calm summer evenings. First gold, then pink, the high glaciers light up in the final minutes of the day, their images mirrored on the surface of Eunice Lake and dozens of other blue gems ringing the sacred mountain.

The central Washington desert has small but significant waterways. A geologist friend once helped me locate a place on a geologic map where a stream seemed to be cutting through sandstone instead of the usual basalt. We both knew from exploring southern Utah how beautiful stream-worn sandstone can be, and the next day, we set off to find it. A dirt road led to the stream, and we hiked along its banks. Soon the creek began to carve its way between canyon walls, cascading in places into small pools, and creating smooth sandstone ledges. It was a great delight to find this little, isolated slickrock area, with its sculpted canyon walls reflecting on the stream's surface.

Water often inspires me to photograph the Washington landscape. It provides an ever-changing palette. Reflections, sometimes razor sharp and at other times abstractly impressionistic, challenge me as I try to see, imagine, and then compose for form and color. When these elements come together, a bit of water's inspiration may be captured on film.

—Charles Gurche
Spokane, Washington

Mount Shuksan, North Cascades National Park

"Every situation — nay, every moment — is of infinite worth, for it is the representative of a whole eternity."

— Goethe, in Eckermann's *Conversations*

Mount Rainier looms over Frozen Lake,
Mount Rainier National Park

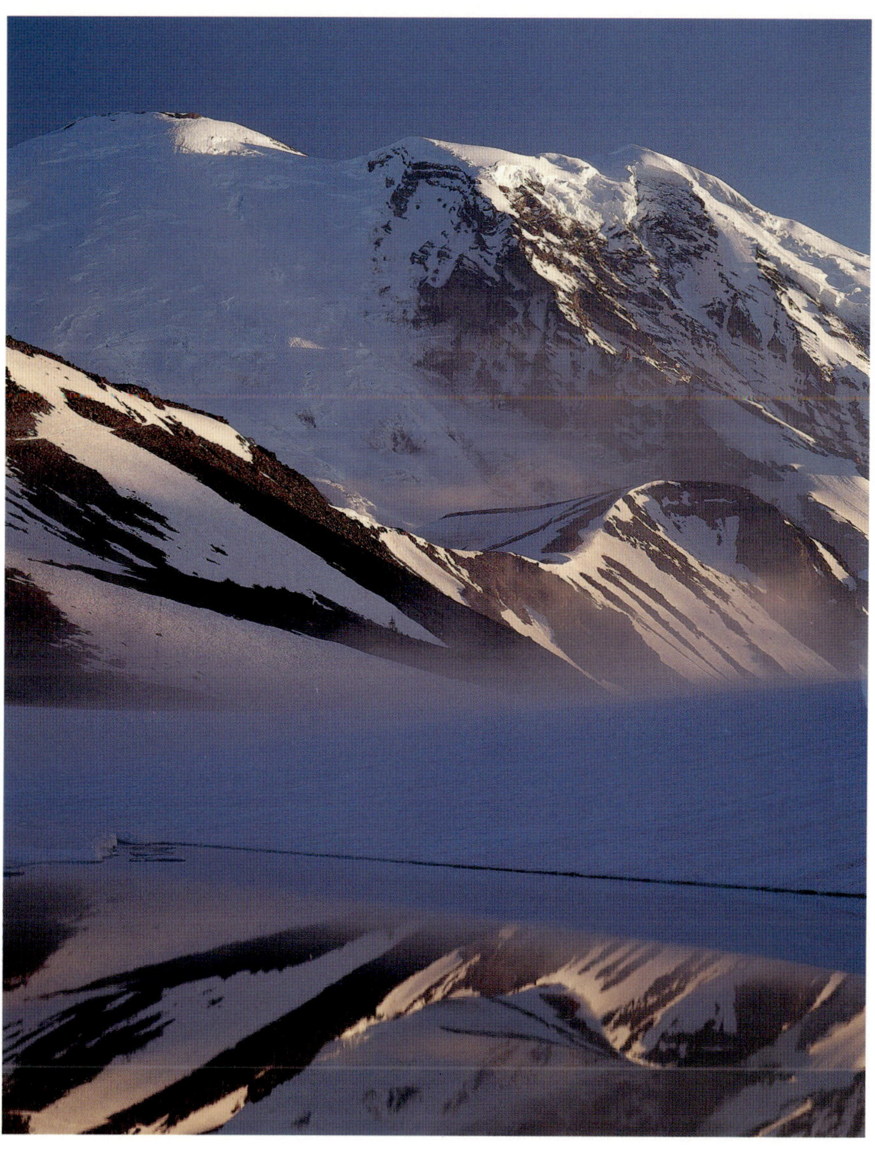

"Come forth into the light of things.
Let Nature be your Teacher."

— William Wordsworth, *The Tables Turned*

Tide pool at sunset, near Copalis Beach

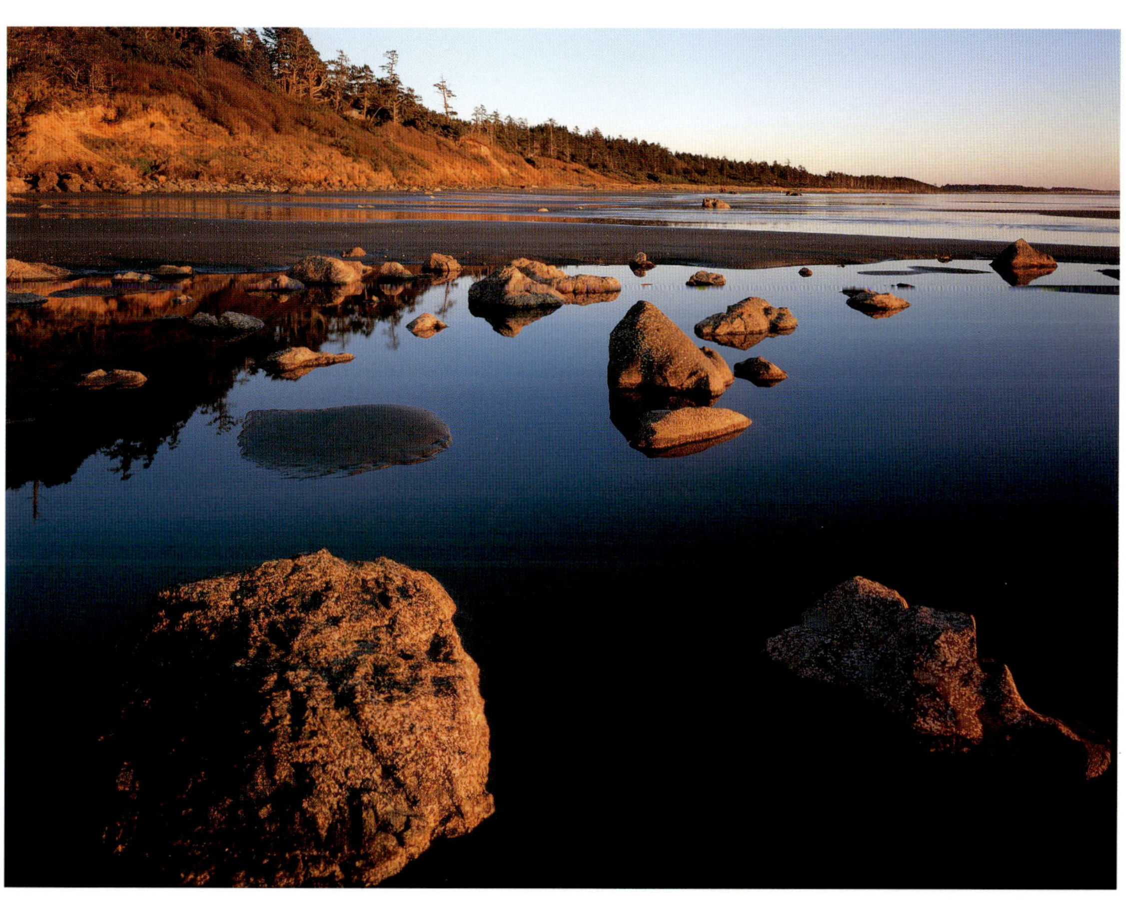

"A taste for the beautiful is most cultivated out of doors..."

— Henry David Thoreau, *Walden*

Lupine reflections, Tipsoo Lake, Mount Rainier National Park

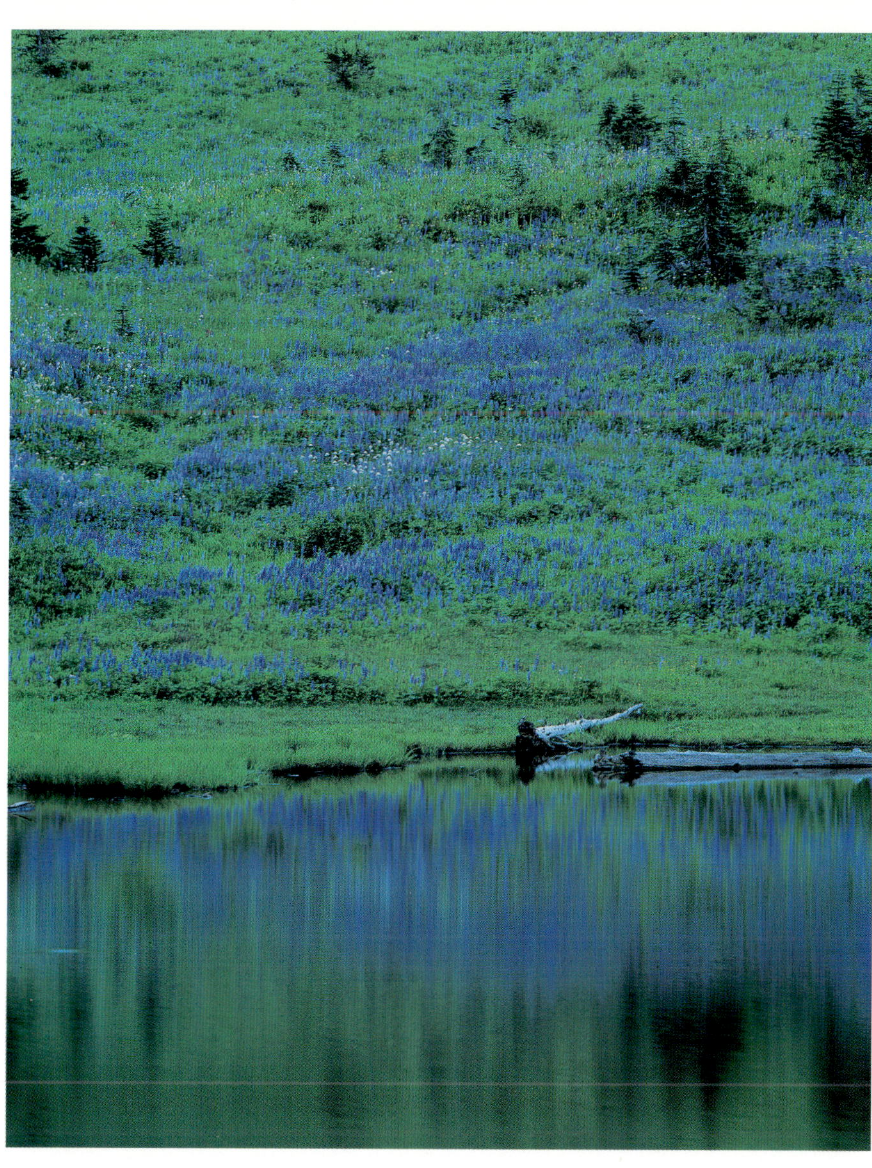

"For in and out, above, about, below,
'Tis nothing but a Magic Shadow-show,
Played in a Box whose Candle is the Sun,
Round which we Phantom Figures come and go."

— Omar Khayyam, *Rubaiyat*

Silhouetted black cottonwood, Spokane River

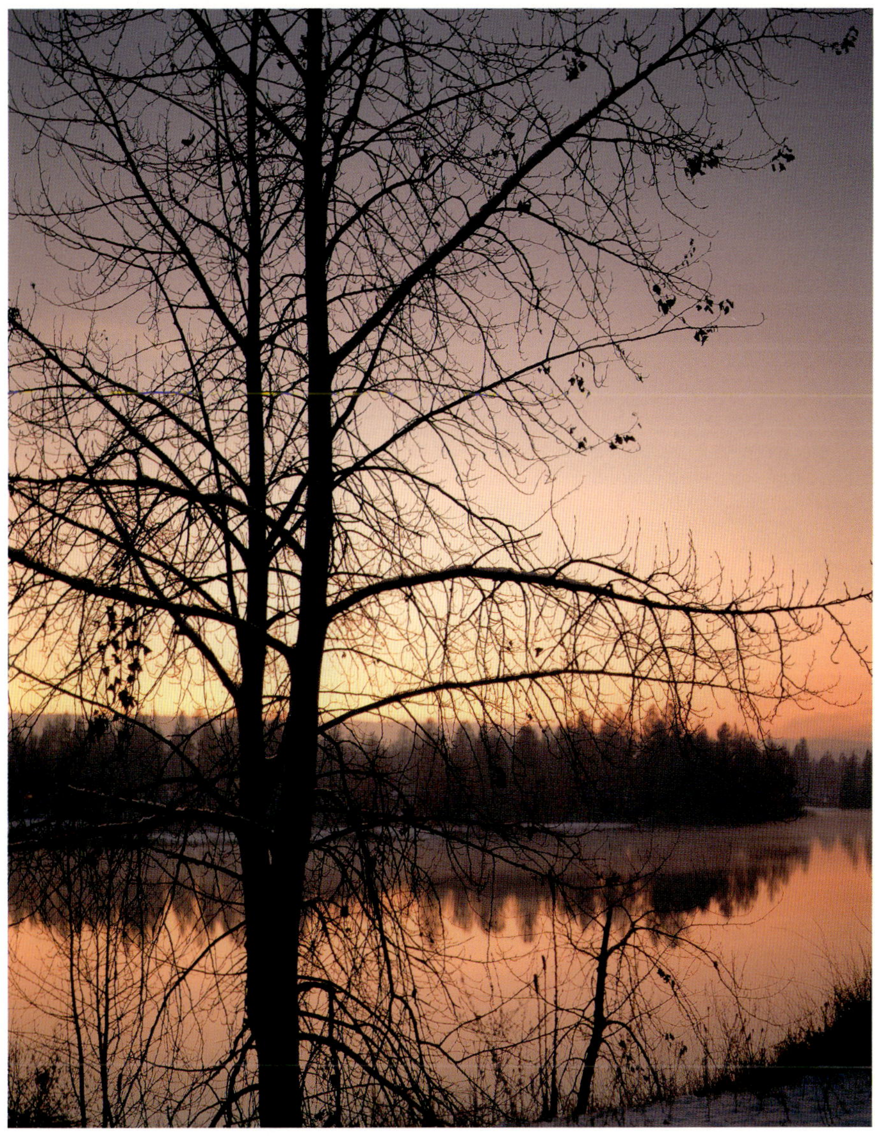

"A rock pile ceases to be a rock pile the moment a single man contemplates it, bearing within him the image of a cathedral."

— Antoine de Saint-Exupery, *Flight to Arras*

Twilight at Copalis Beach

Overleaf: Lupine and evergreens, William O. Douglas Wilderness

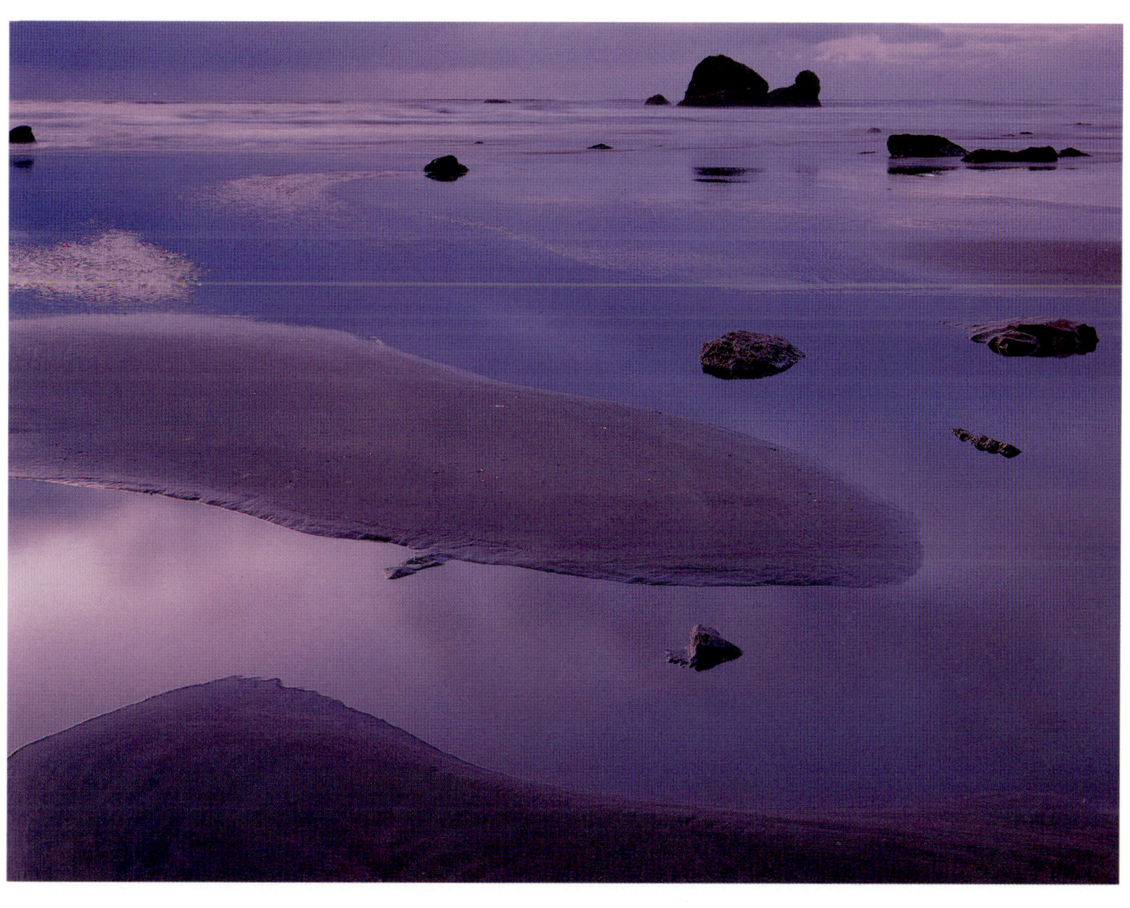

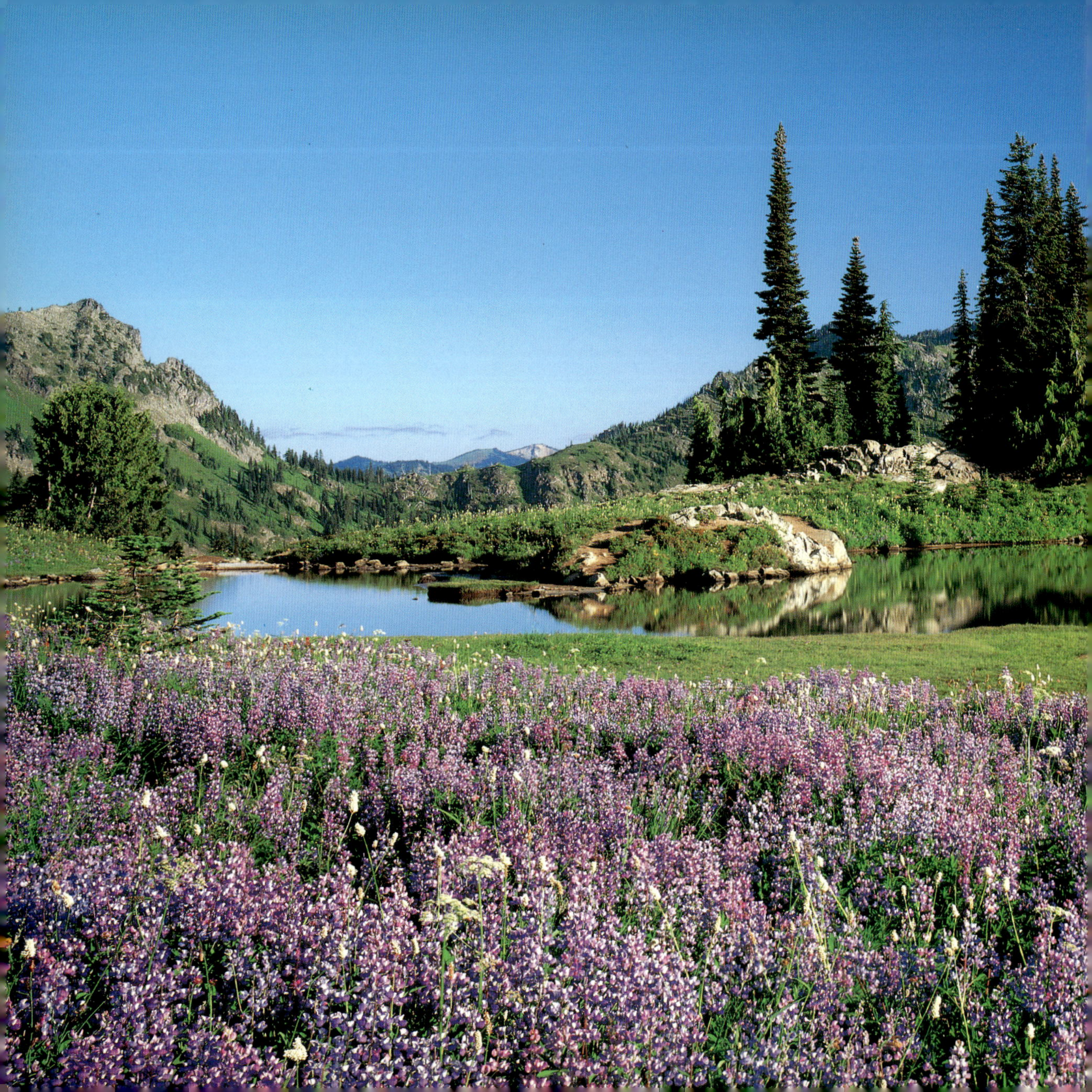

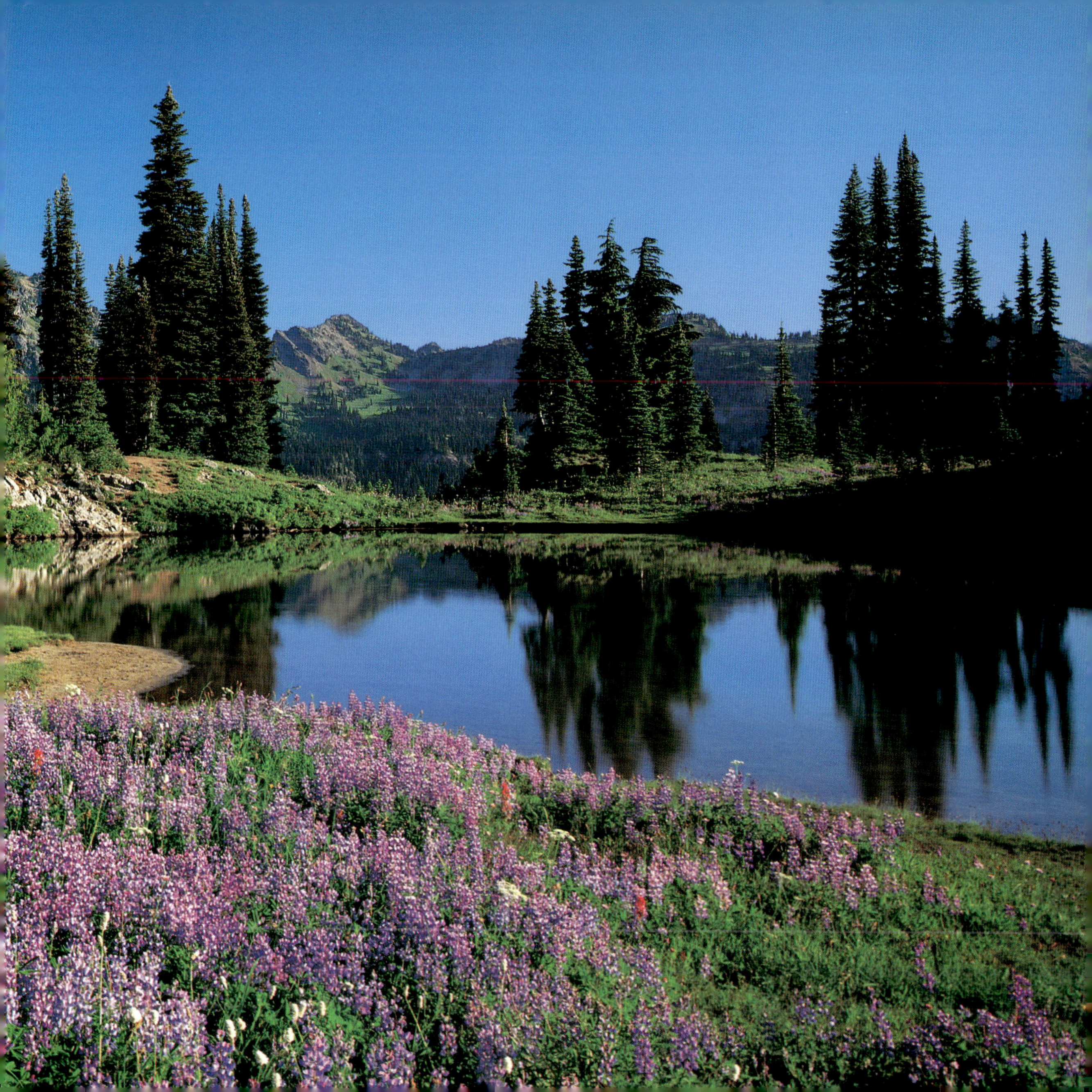

"There is a road from the eye to the heart
that does not go through the intellect."

— G. K. Chesterton, *The Defendant*

Reflection Lake, Mount Rainier National Park

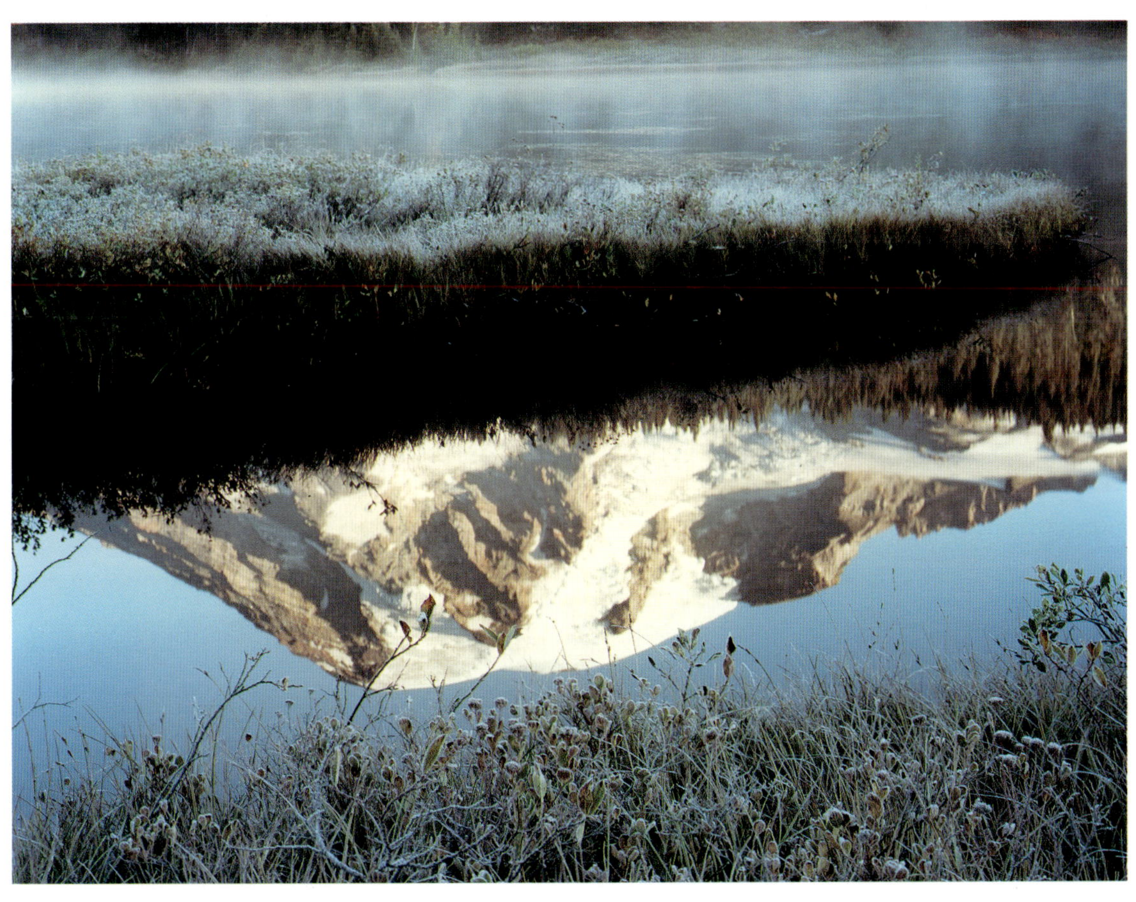

"It is the marriage of the soul with Nature that makes the intellect fruitful, and gives birth to the imagination."

— Henry David Thoreau, *Journal*

Elwha River, Olympic National Park

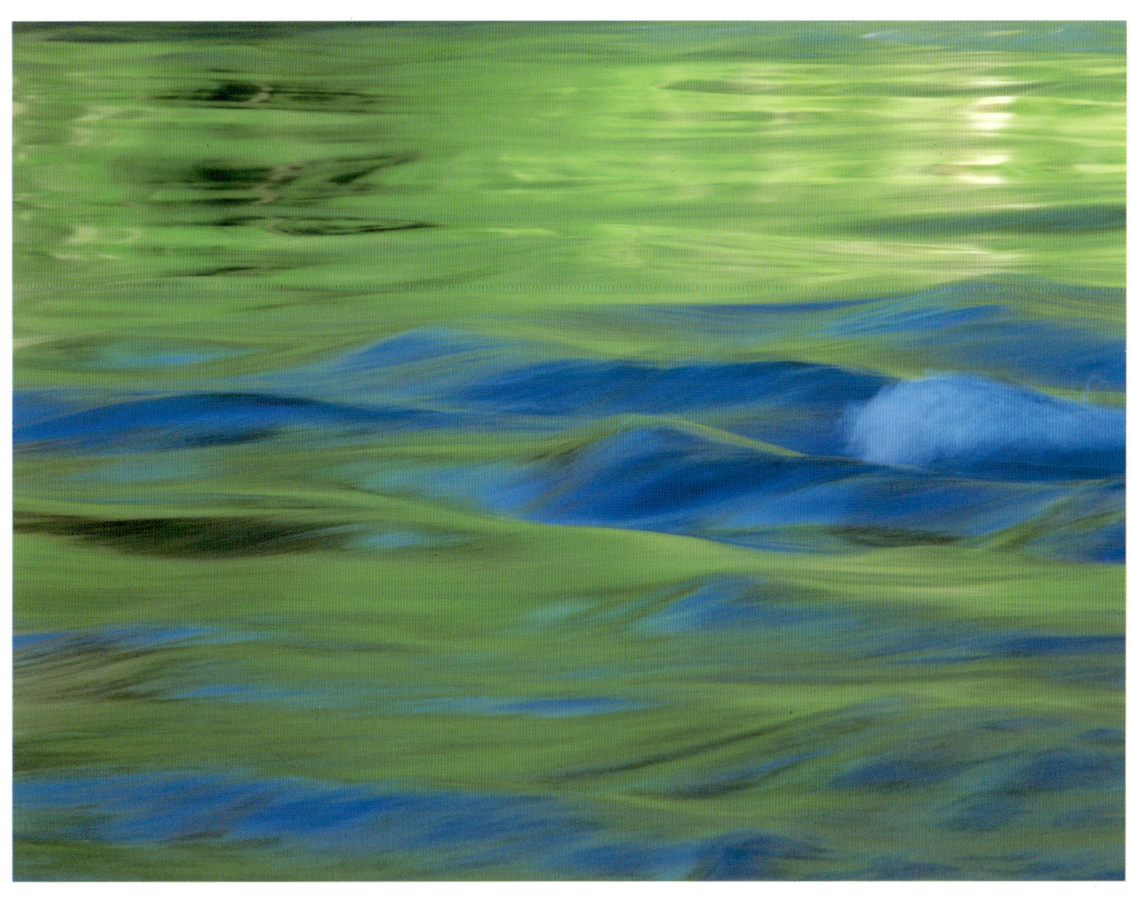

"The day, water, sun, moon, night — I do not have to purchase these things with money."

— Titus Maccius Plautus, *The Comedy of Asses*

Moon above ponderosa pines, Granite Lake, Spokane County

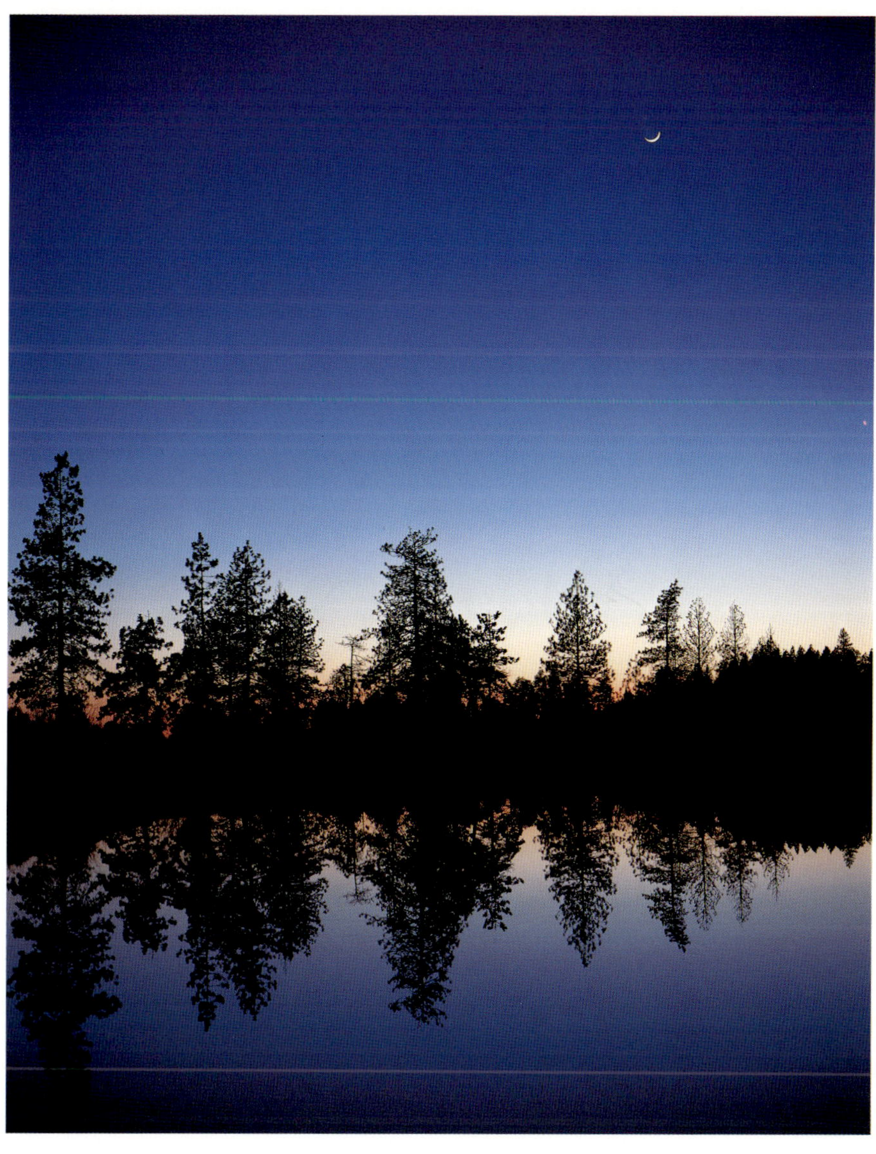

"We need the tonic of wildness...
We can never have enough of nature
We must be refreshed by the sight of inexhaustible vigor,
vast and titanic features..."

— Henry David Thoreau, *Walden*

Lake Brynhild, Alpine Lakes Wilderness

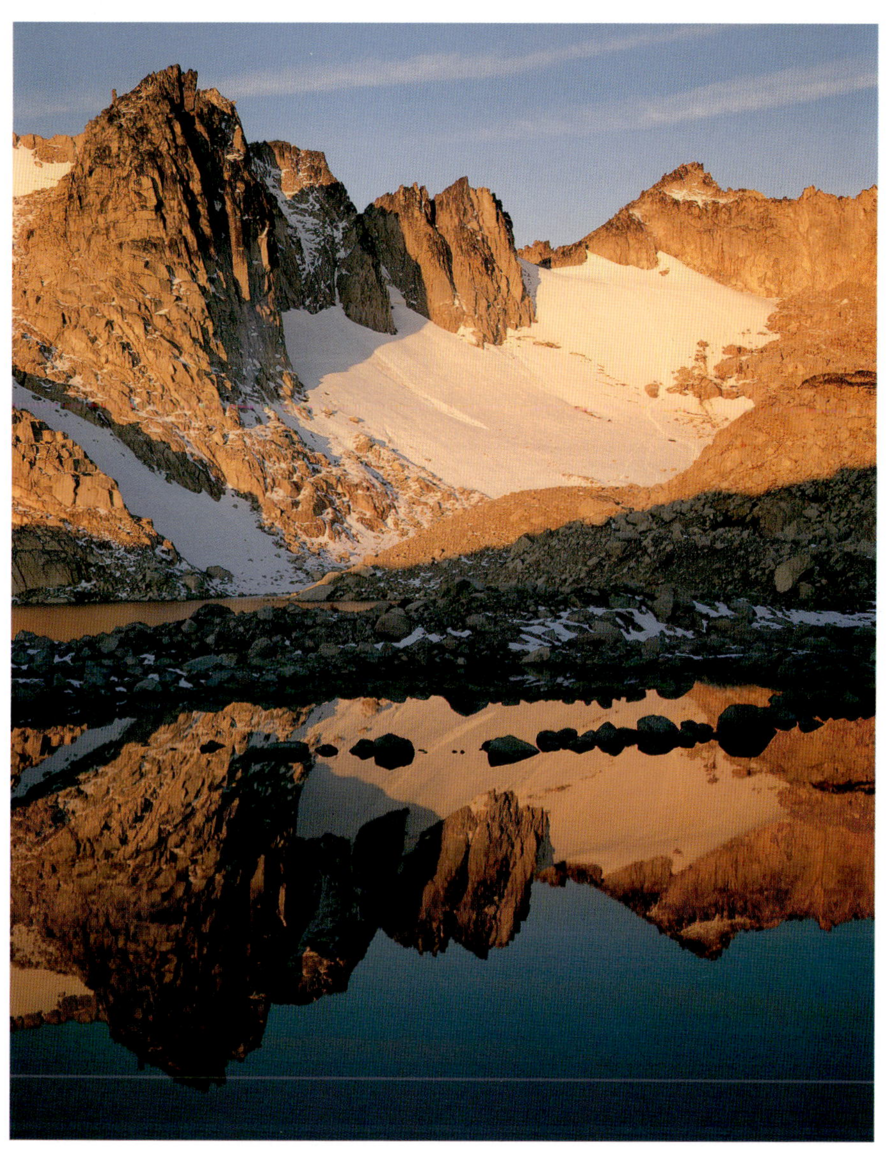

"In Nature's infinite book of secrecy,
A little I can read."

— Shakespeare, *Antony and Cleopatra*

Second Beach at dawn, Olympic National Park

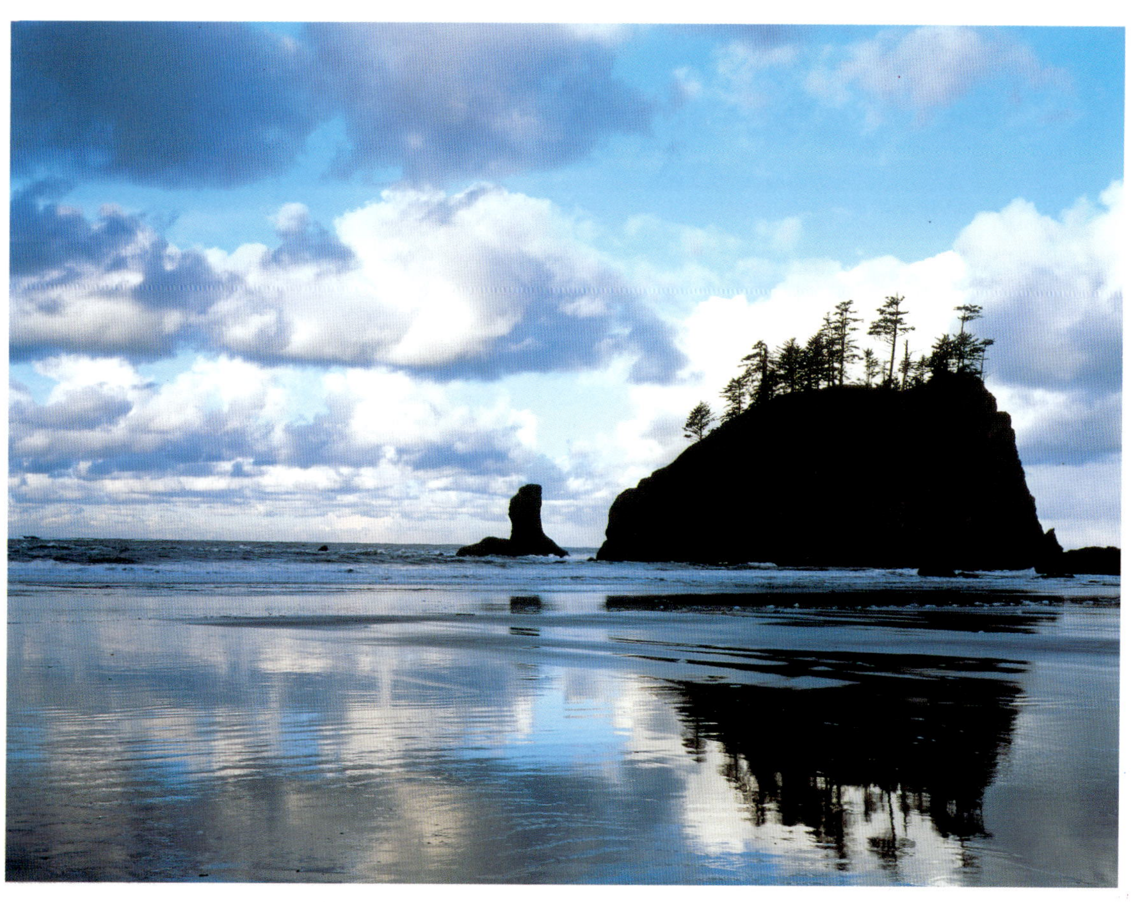

"To the attentive eye, each moment of the year
has its own beauty…it beholds, every hour,
a picture which was never seen before,
and which shall never be seen again."

— Ralph Waldo Emerson, *Beauty*

Autumn huckleberry, Reflection Lake, Mount Rainier National Park

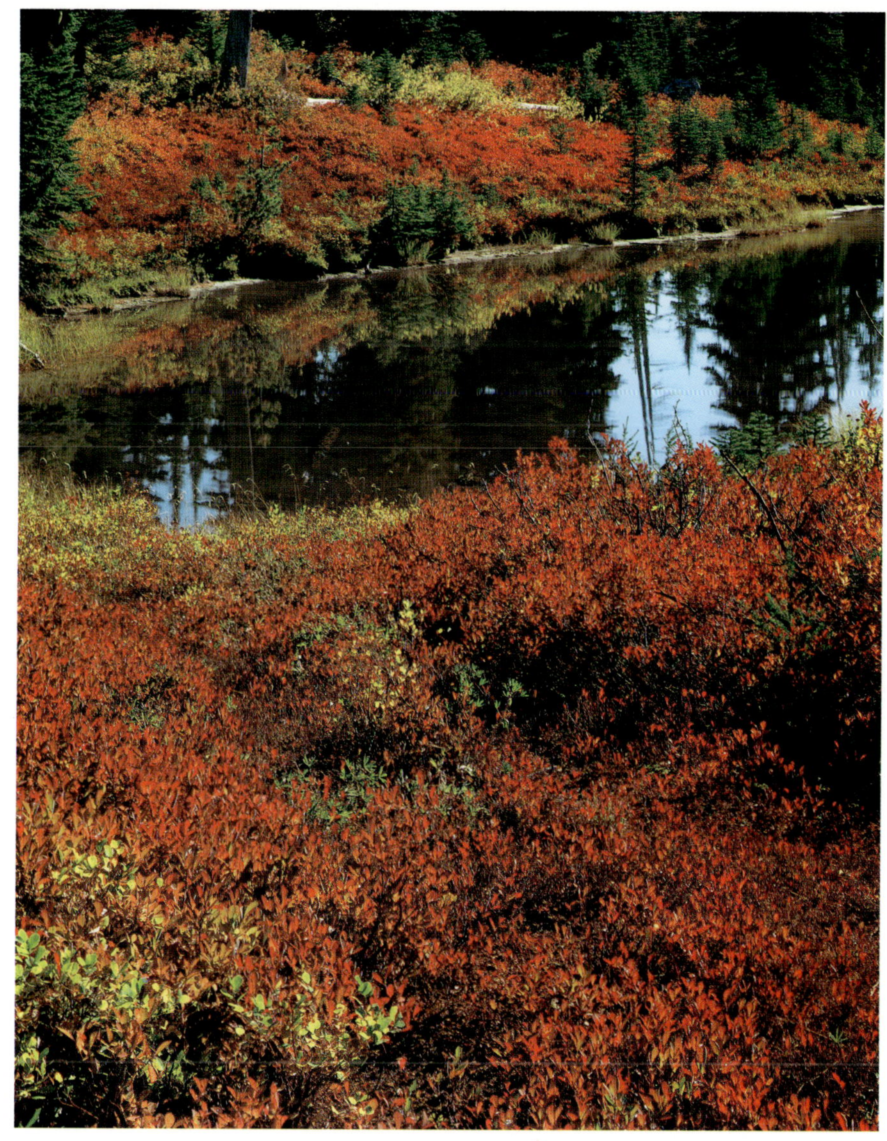

"Everybody needs beauty as well as bread, places to play in and pray in where Nature may heal and cheer and give strength to the body and soul alike."

— John Muir, *Travels in Alaska*

Wind patterns in snow, Philleo Lake, Spokane County

Overleaf: Sunset, Granite Lake, Spokane County

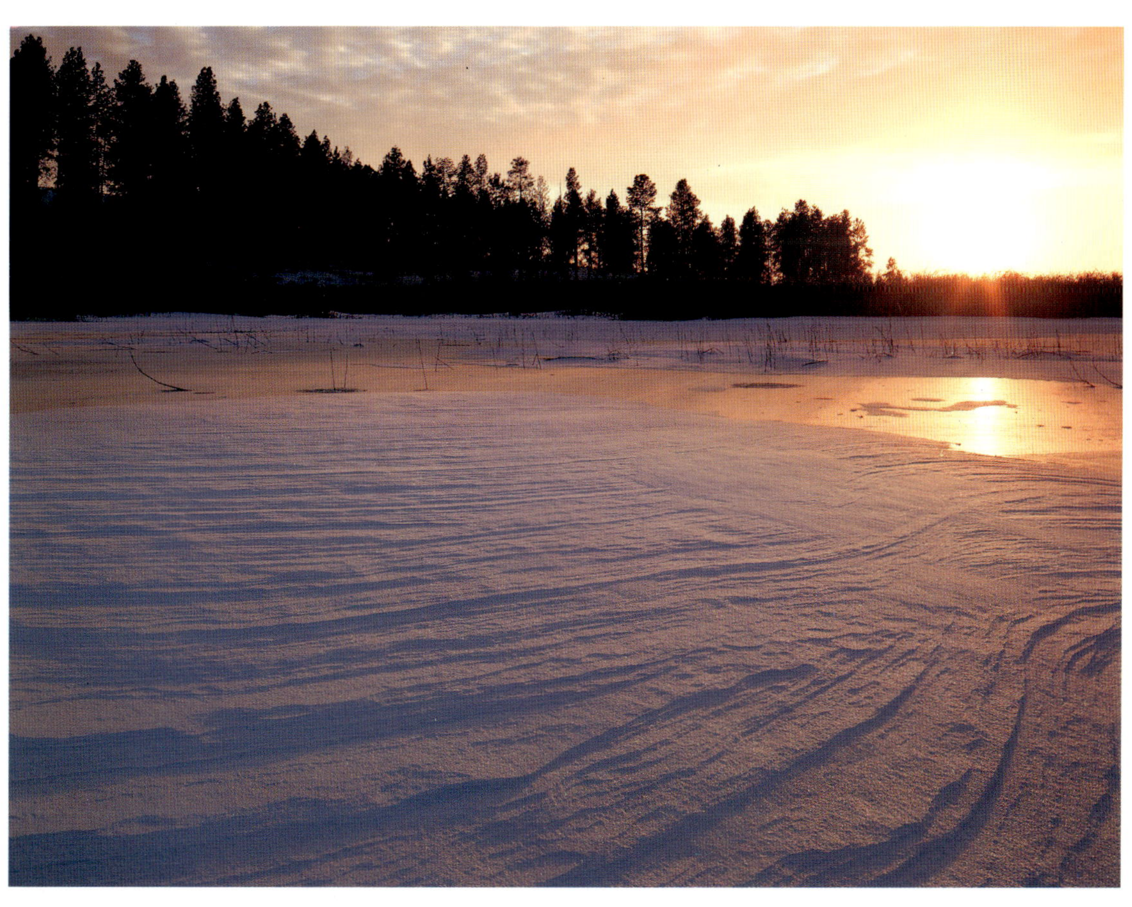

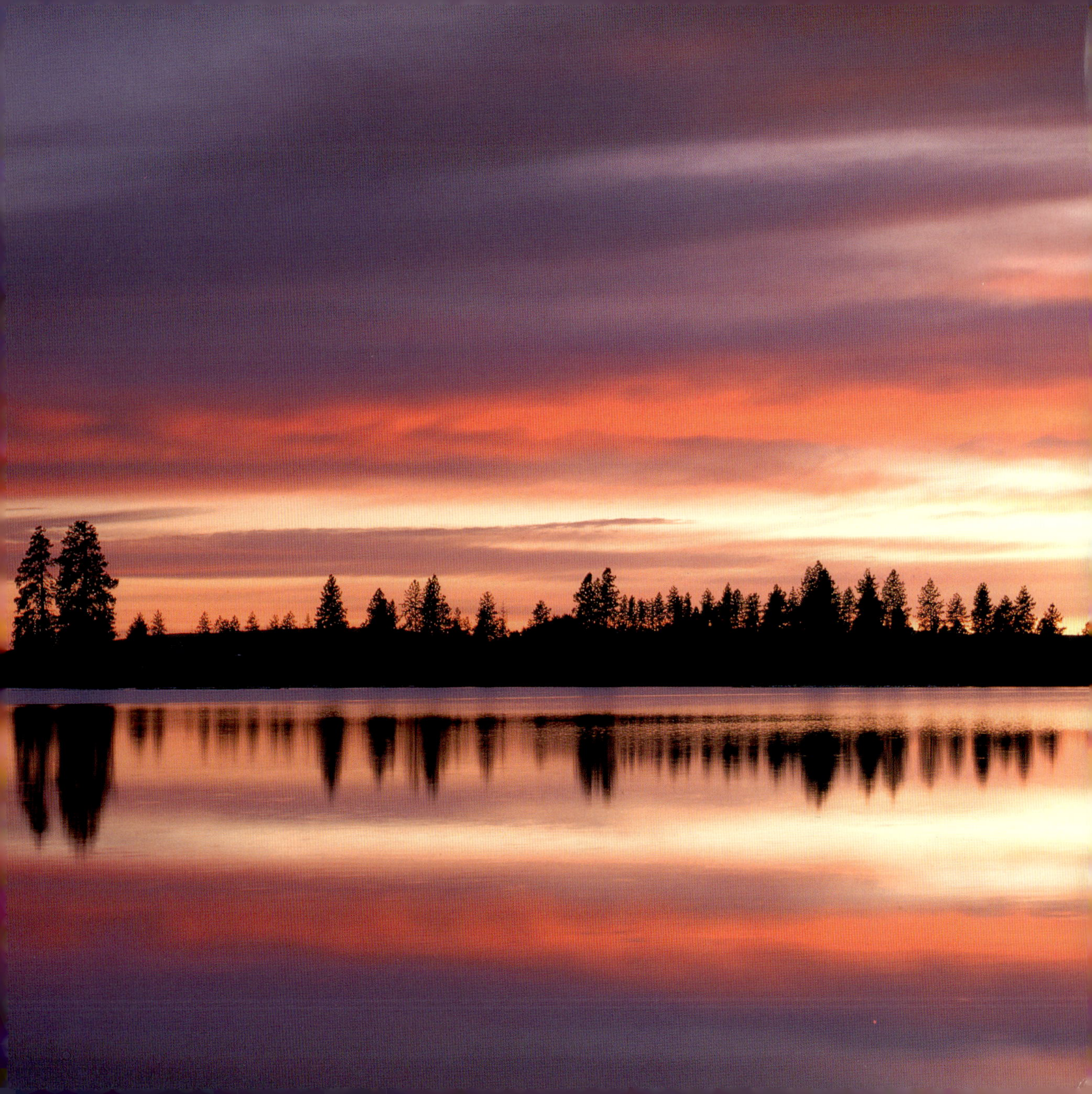

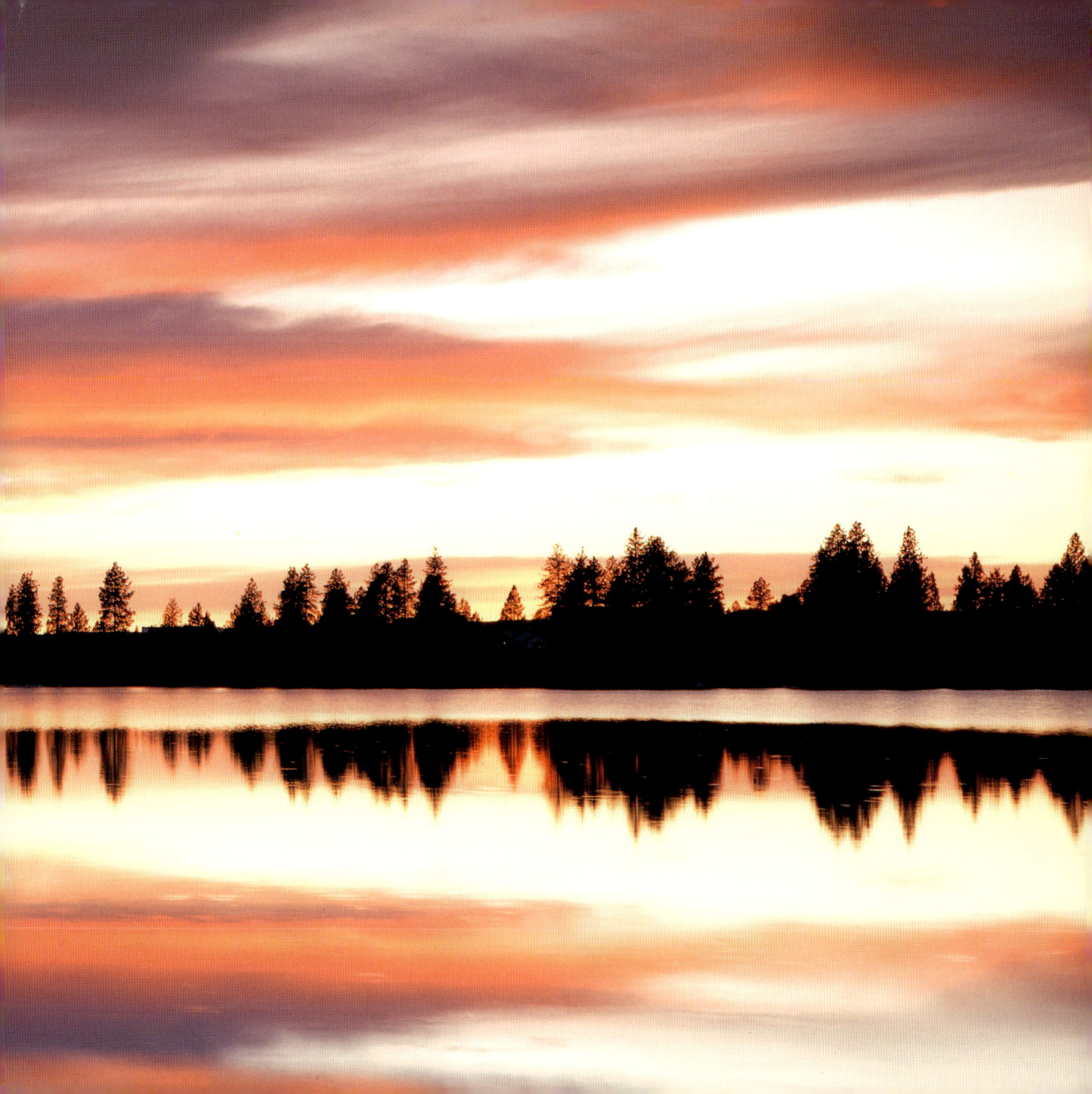

"The whole secret of the study of nature lies in learning how to use one's eyes..."

— George Sand, *Nouvelles Lettres d'un Voyageur*

Reflections in Tipsoo Lake, Mount Rainier National Park

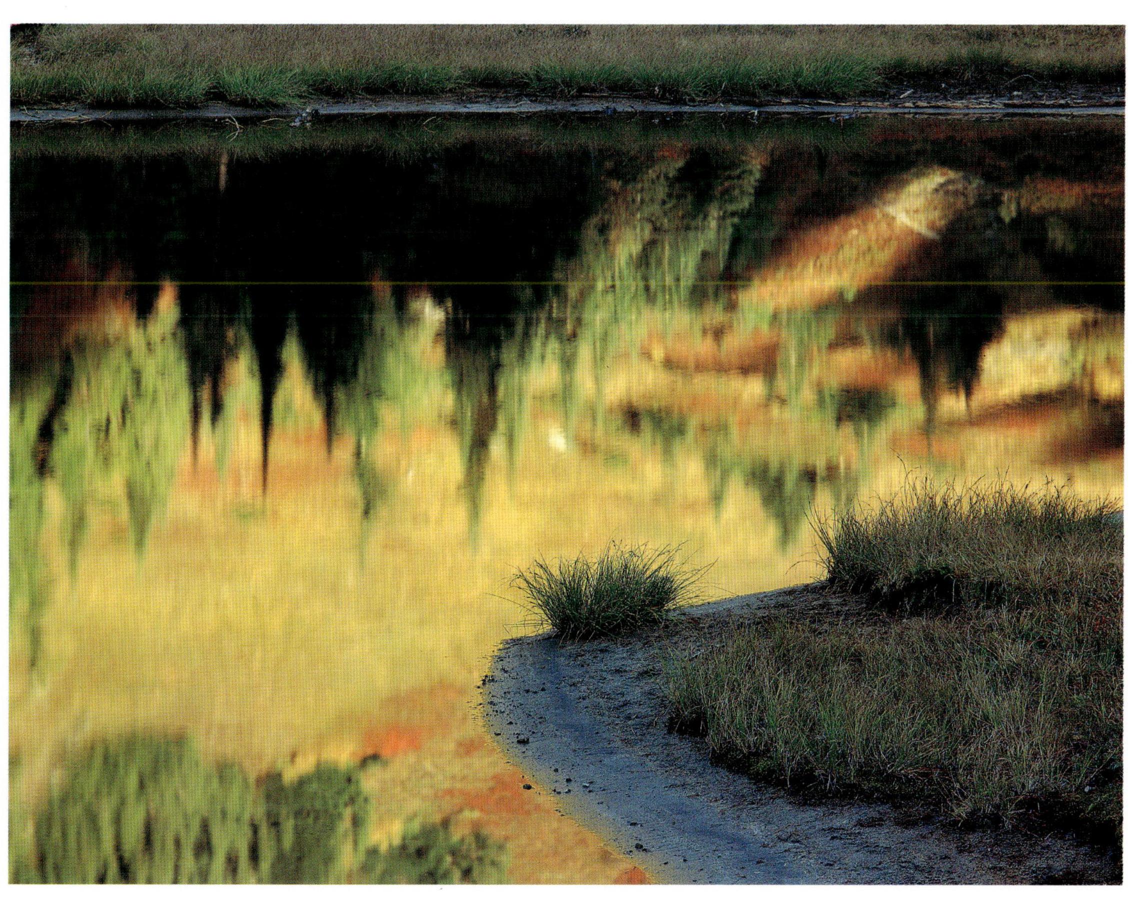

"Everything that happens happens as it should, and if you observe carefully, you will find this to be so."

— Marcus Aurelius, *Meditations*

Eunice Lake below Mount Rainier, Mount Rainier National Park

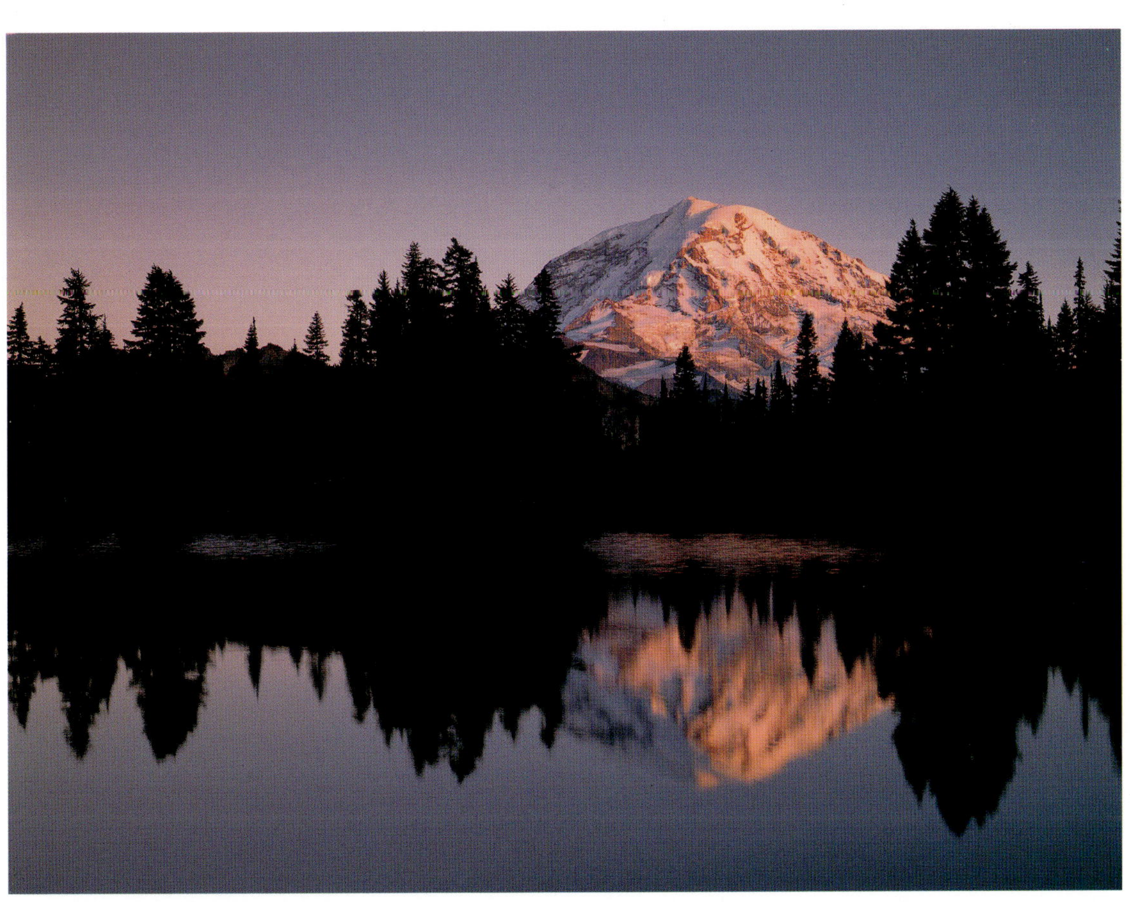

"Nature is an endless combination and repetition of a very few laws. She hums the old well-known air through innumerable variations."

— Ralph Waldo Emerson, *Essays*

Snowfield, Mount Baker Wilderness

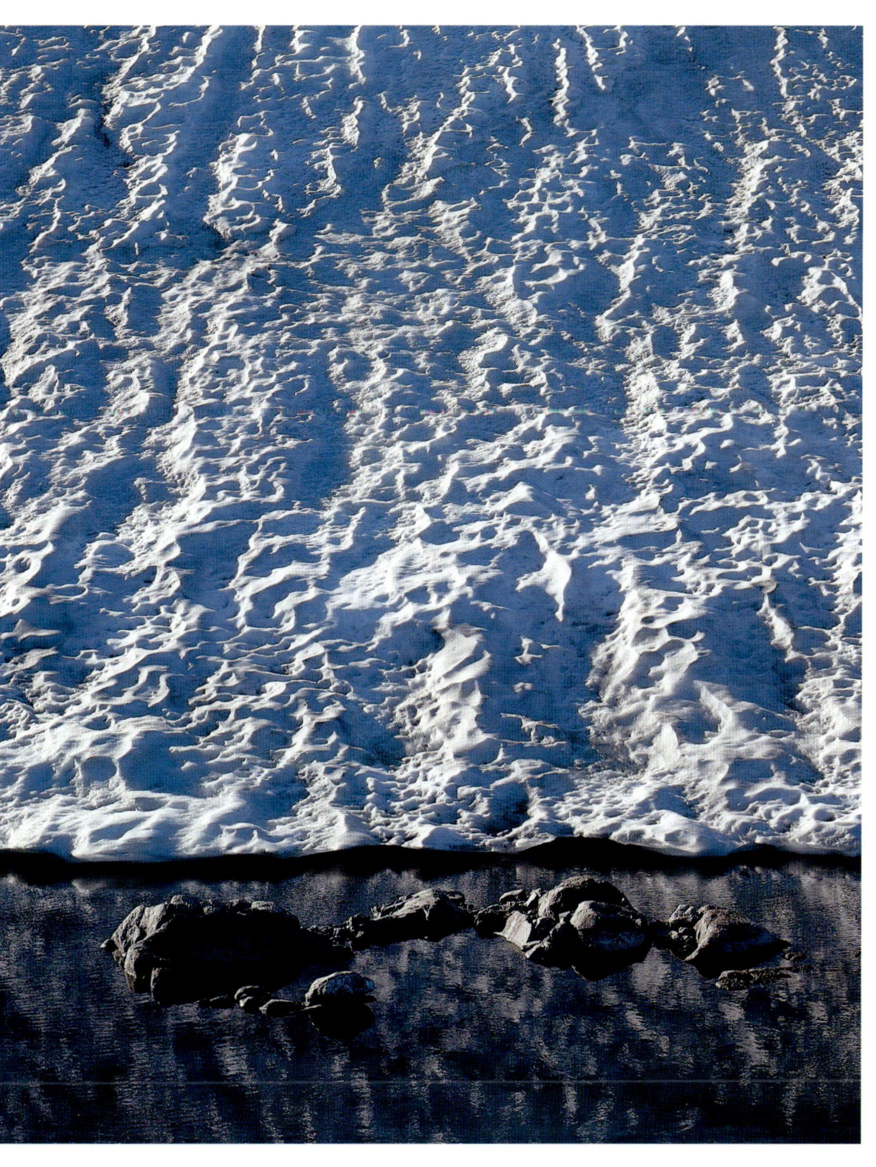

"The world turns softly
Not to spill its lakes and rivers,
The water is held in its arms
And the sky is held in the water.
What is water, that pours silver,
And can hold the sky?"

— Hilda Conkling, *Water*

Larch trees in autumn, Alpine Lakes Wilderness

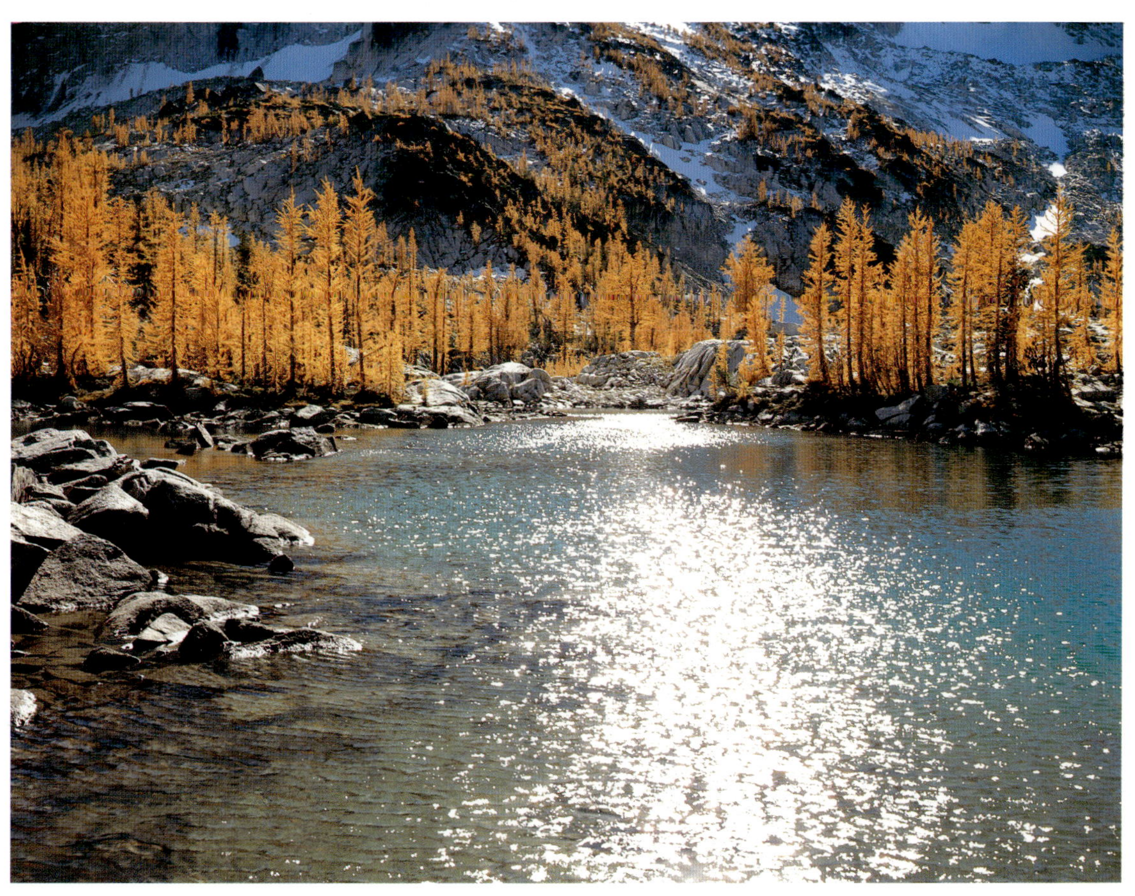

"Nature has presented us with a large faculty of entertaining ourselves alone...to teach us that we owe ourselves in part to society, but chiefly and mostly to ourselves."

— Montaigne, *On Giving the Lie*

Sunrise and clouds, Griffin Bay, San Juan Island

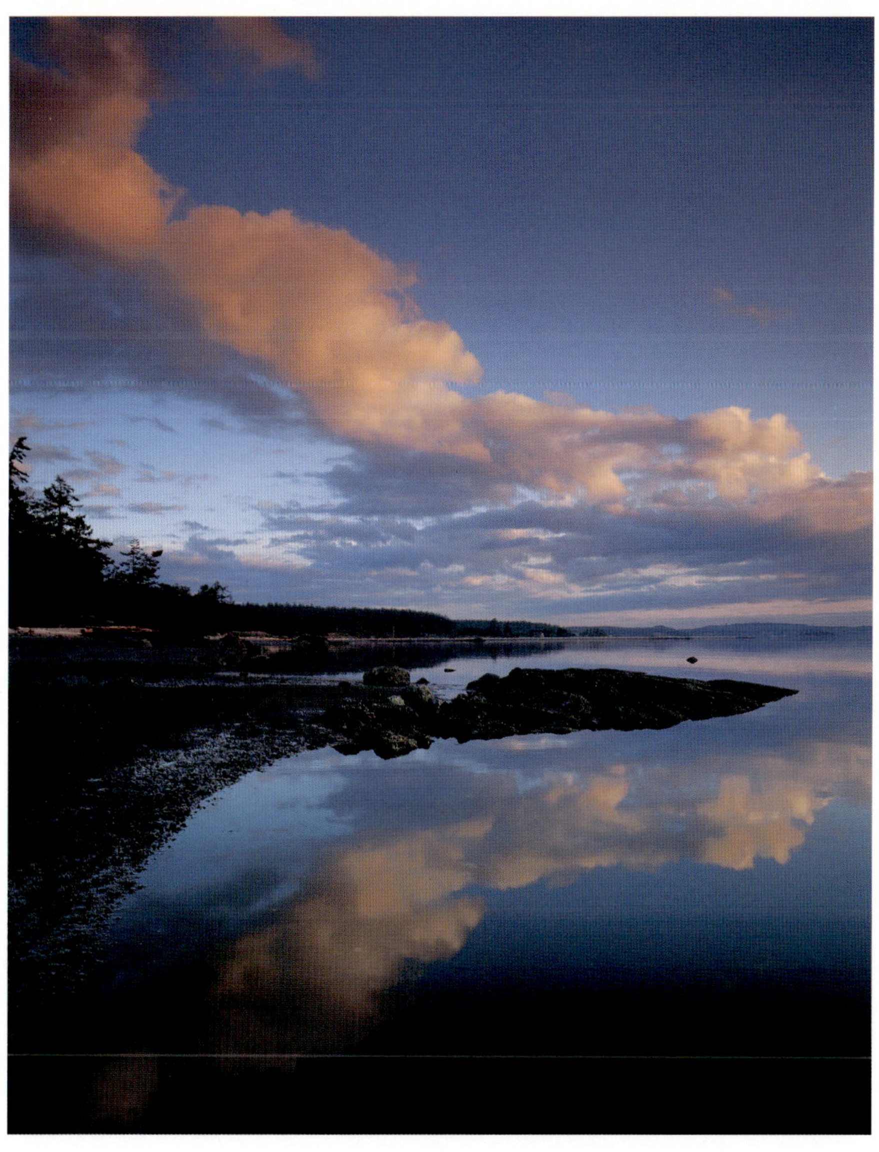

“How often we forget all time, when lone
Admiring Nature’s universal throne
Her woods, her wilds, her waters intense
Reply of hers to our intelligence.”

— Lord Byron, *The Island*

Alder forest, Olympic National Park

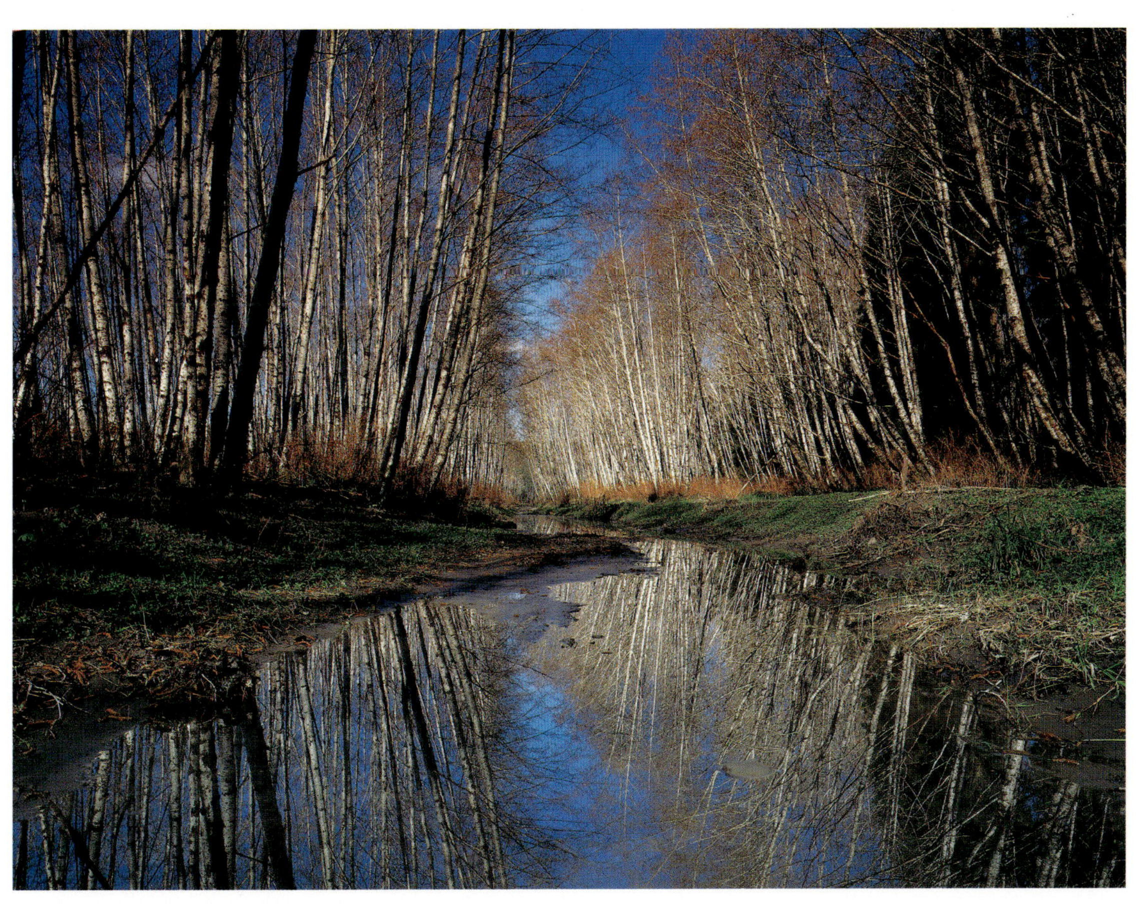

"We do not receive wisdom,
we have to discover it for ourselves
by a voyage that no one can take for us..."

— Marcel Proust, *Remembrance of Things Past*

Ohanapecosh River, Mount Rainier National Park

Overleaf: Sea stacks, Second Beach, Olympic National Park

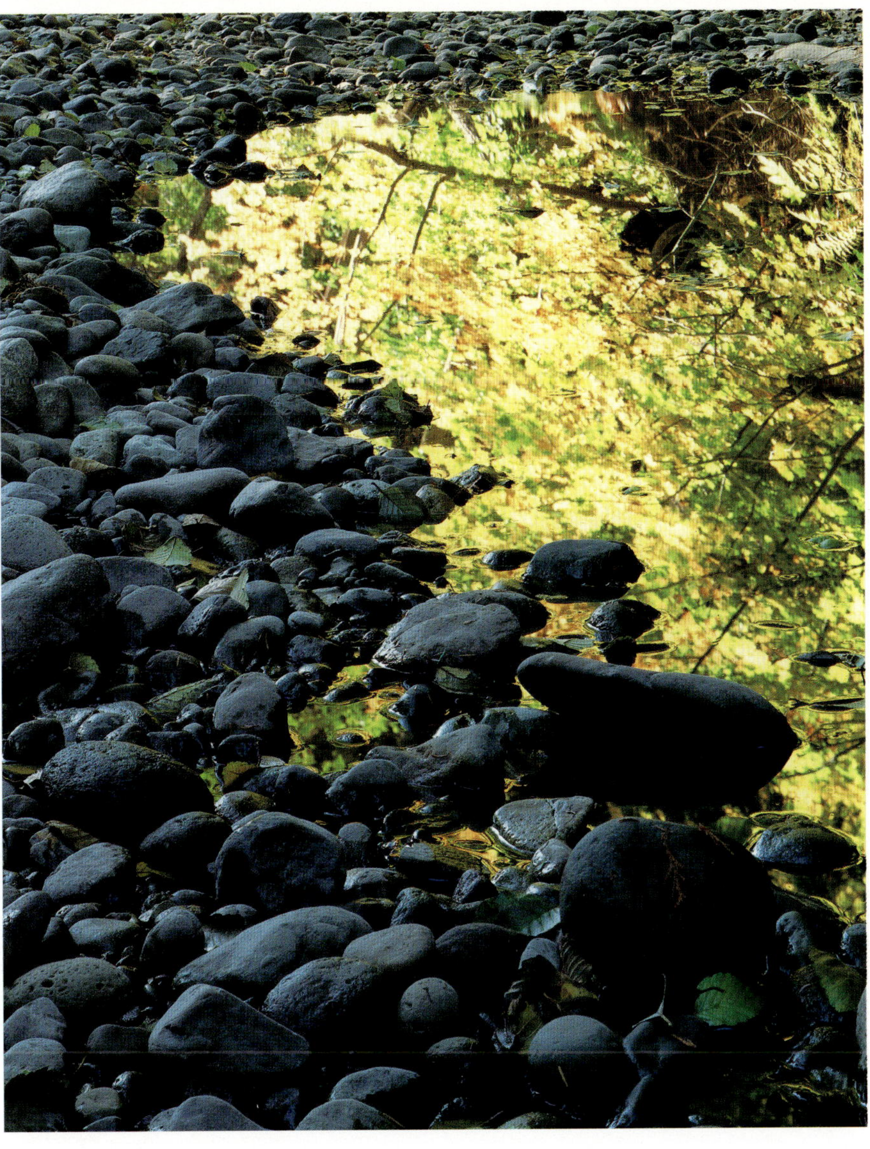

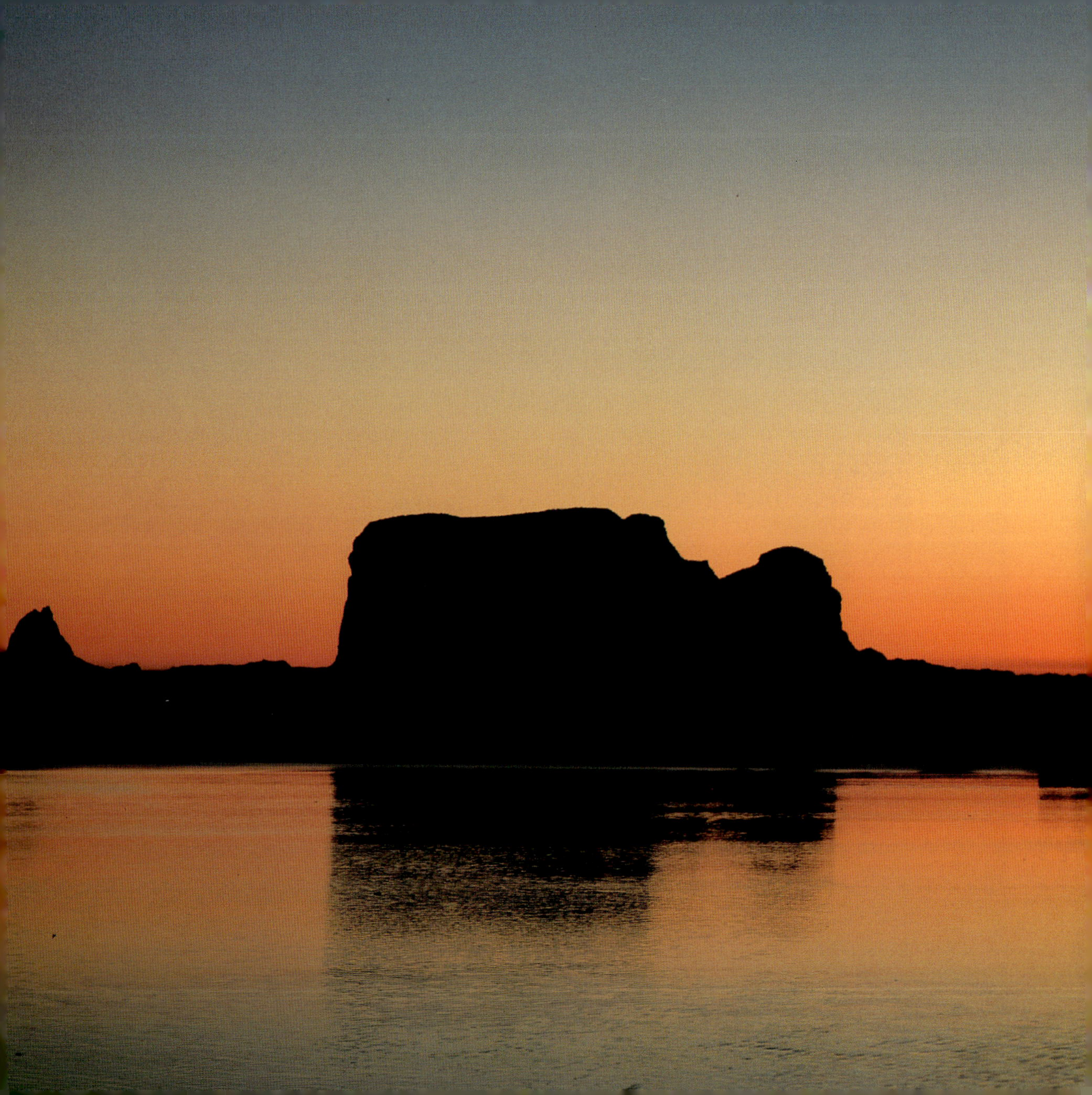

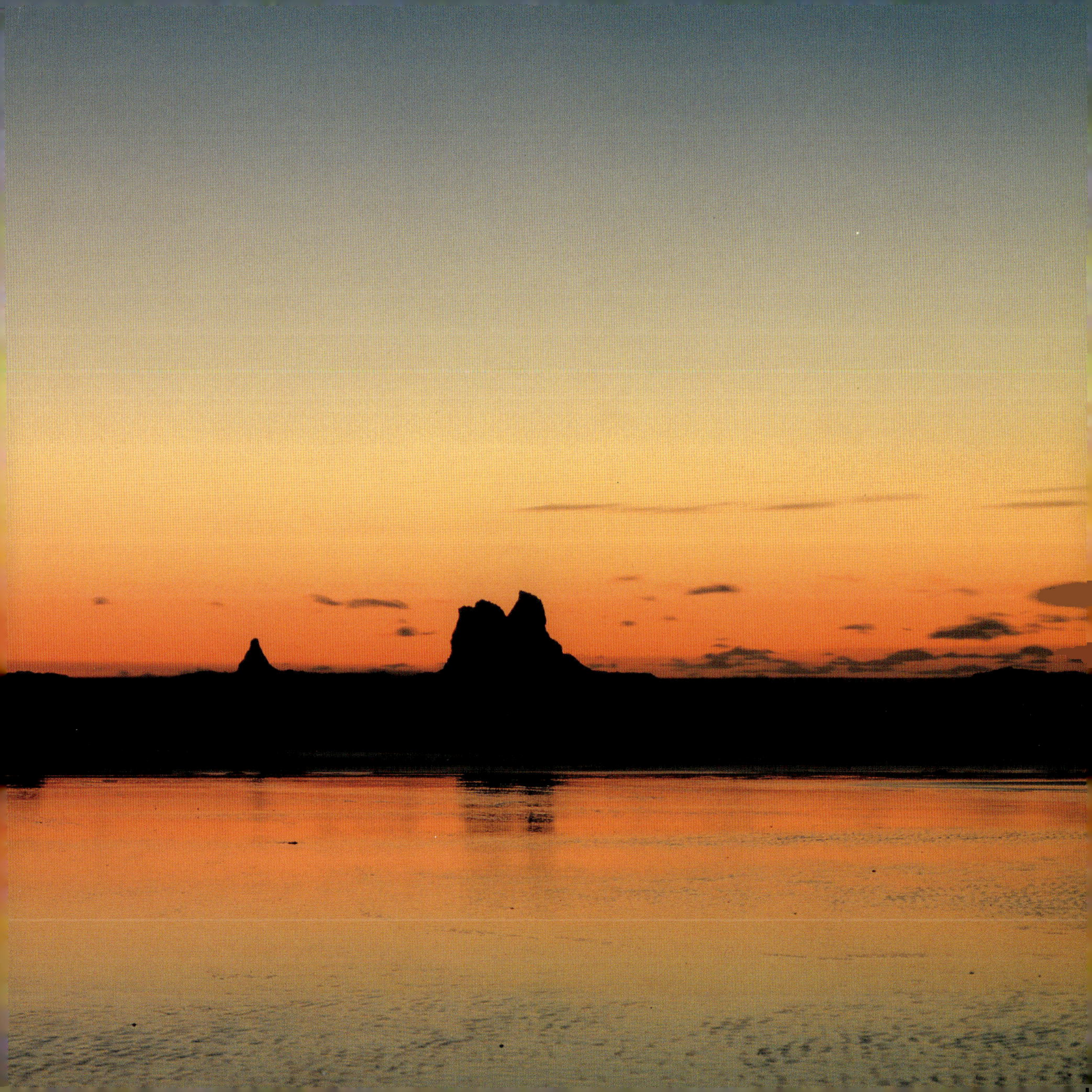

“Surely there is something in the unruffled calm of nature that overawes our little anxieties and doubts; the sight of the deep-blue sky...seems to impart a quiet to the mind.”

— Jonathan Edwards, *The New Dictionary of Thoughts*

Icebergs, Bagley Creek, Cascade Range

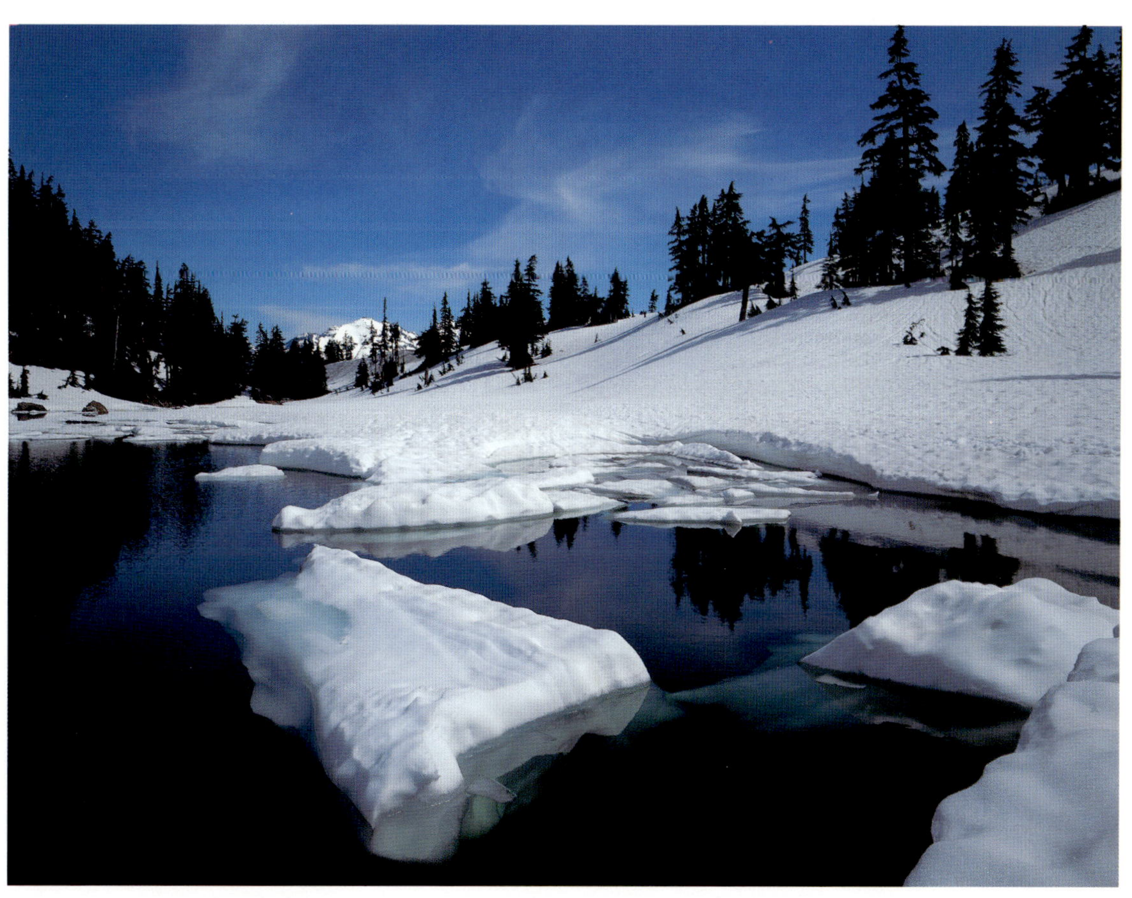

"To him who in the love of Nature holds
Communion with her visible forms, she speaks
A various language."

—William Cullen Bryant, *Thanatopsis*

Alder tree along the Elwha River, Olympic National Park

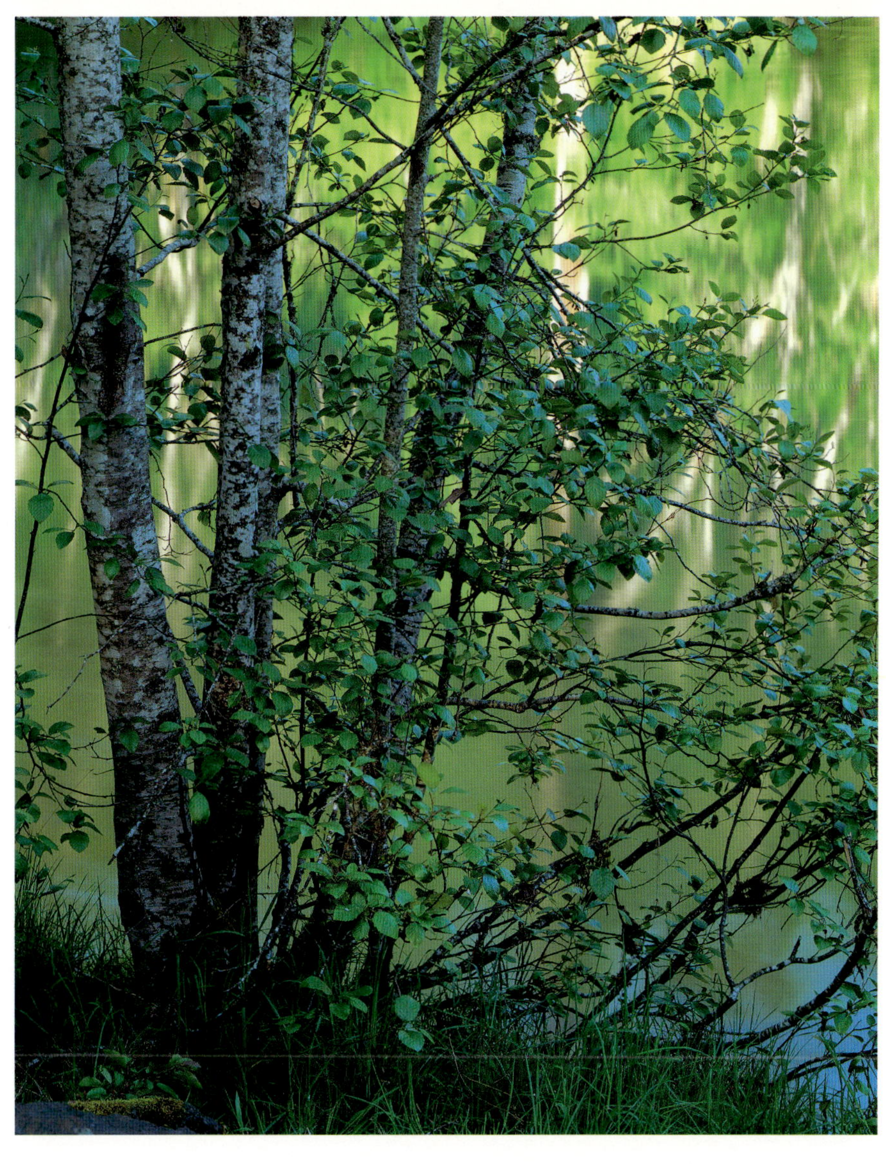

"Solitude...is essential to any depth of meditation or of character; and solitude in the presence of natural beauty and grandeur, is the cradle of thoughts and aspirations..."

— John Stuart Mill, *Principles of Political Economy*

Ice crystals, Banks Lake, Steamboat Rock State Park

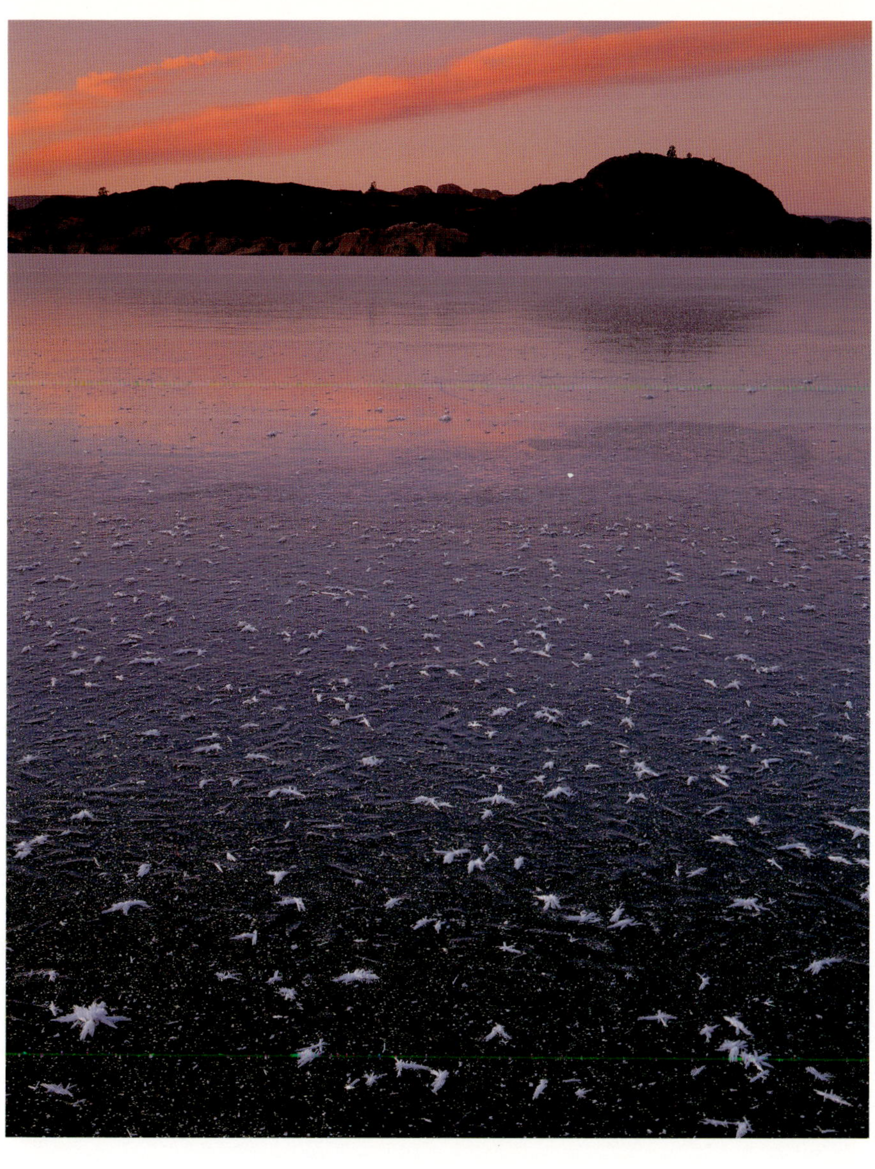

"Let us permit nature to have her way:
she understands her business better than we do."

— Montaigne, *Essays III*

Mount Shuksan reflected in Picture Lake,
North Cascades National Park

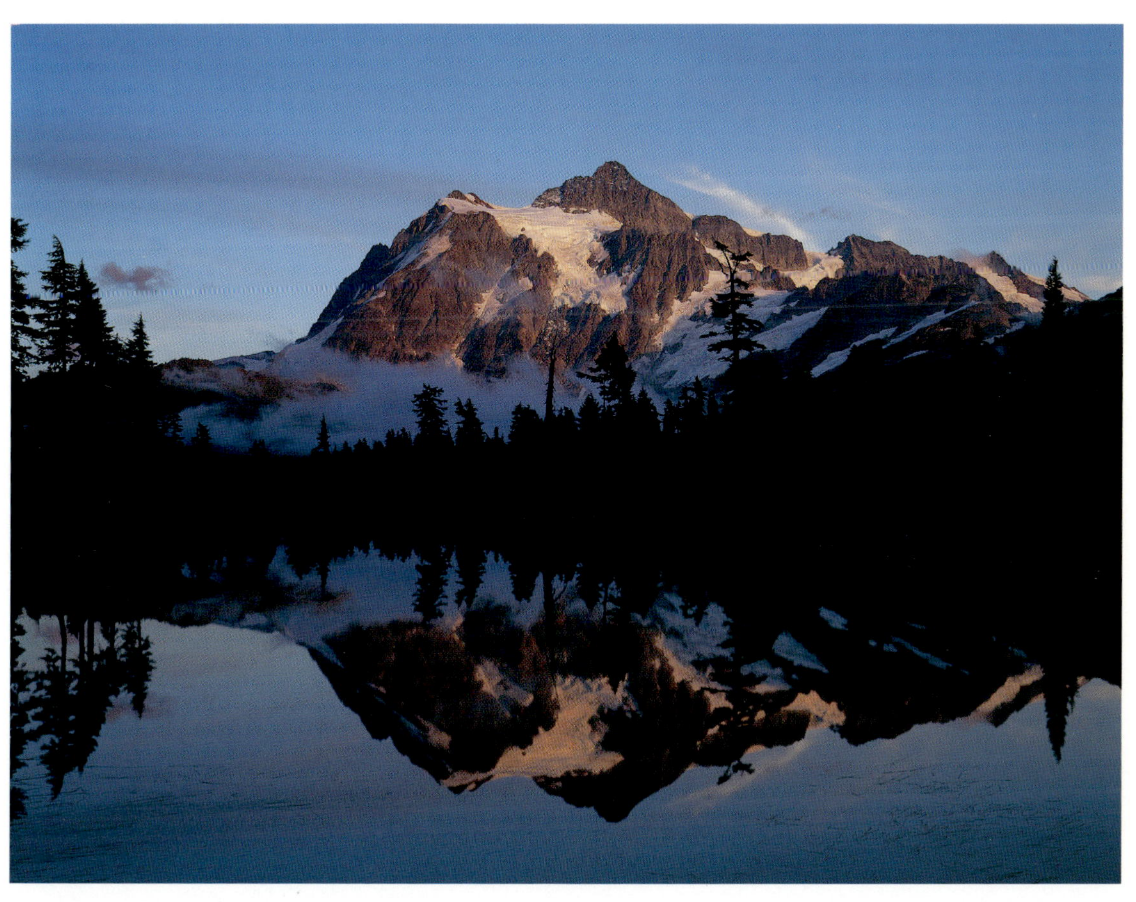

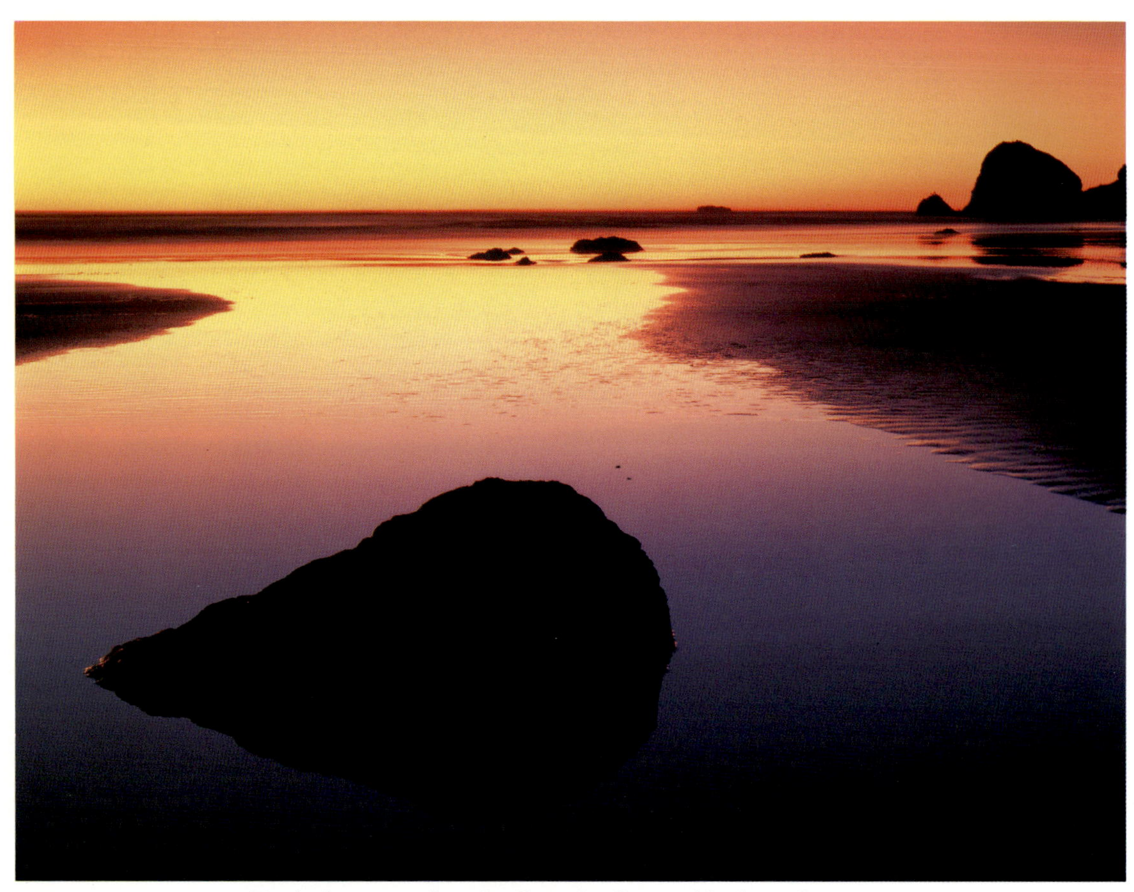

Twilight, near Pacific Beach, Grays Harbor County